Inside Taekwondo

Inside Taekwondo

A Collection of Articles on the Mental Aspects of Taekwondo & other Martial Arts

Sean Pearson

Copyright © 2012 by Sean Pearson

All rights reserved. This book or any portion thereof
May not be reproduced or used in any manner whatsoever
Without the express written permission of the publisher
Except for the use of brief quotations in a book review.

Printed in the United States of America

First Printing, 2012

ISBN-13: 978-0615732381 (New Tiger Publications)
ISBN-10: 0615732380

Shin Ho Kwan
Rochester, New York

www.ShinHoKwan.org
ShinHoKwan@me.com

To my Instructors:

Grandmaster Kyongwon Ahn
Onyumishi Kanjuro Shibata XX
Grandmaster Nonoy Gallano

Thank you for giving your knowledge so willingly
and for putting up with my ignorance for so many years.

Acknowledgments

Throughout this book, I often mention three of my instructors: Grandmaster Kyongwon Ahn, Onyumishi Kanjuro Shibata XX Sensei and Grandmaster Nonoy Gallano. If it were not for these individuals' unrelenting pursuit of their martial arts, this book would not have been possible. I owe them everything.

Grandmaster Kyongwon Ahn

Grandmaster Kyongwon Ahn was born in Seoul, Korea. His training in the martial arts began when he was only twelve years old and continued through his residence in Korea. He served an internship with his instructor, Master Chang Bok Lee, as the Master Instructor for the American and Korean armies from 1955 through 1967. Upon the request of the United States, he immigrated to Cincinnati, Ohio to begin instruction in Taekwondo in August 1967. At this time, he founded the United Taekwondo Association to ensure reputable martial arts instruction in the U.S. In 1968, Grandmaster Ahn began instruction at the University of Cincinnati, where he still serves as an advisor. He has also taught at Miami University of Ohio and Xavier University. During the 1970's, when Taekwondo was beginning its climb to national and international prominence, Grandmaster Ahn was a member of the initial Board of Directors of the National AAU Taekwondo Committee (now the United States Taekwondo Union).

From 1986 until the end of 1992 he served as President of the U.S. Taekwondo Union.

Besides these activities and Grandmaster Ahn's Presidency of the United Taekwondo Association, he has served as the Chairman of the Ohio AAU Taekwondo Committee, Acting Chairman of the National AAU Taekwondo Promotion Committee, and head of the U.S. Team at the 3rd World Taekwondo Championships in 1977. As a 9th degree black belt, Grandmaster Kyong Won Ahn is licensed and accredited by the World Taekwondo Federation as an International Referee and Master Instructor. He is widely known and respected throughout the nation and internationally as a leading figure in Taekwondo, and as a tireless organizer and a dedicated master teacher.

Grandmaster Ahn has trained over 500 black belts, including some to the level of Master, and over 15,000 students. Many of his students have received national recognition in competition and international recognition for their instructor and refereeing skills.

Onyumishi Kanjuro Shibata XX

Onyumishi Kanjuro Shibata is a 20th generation master bowmaker and archer, and 3rd generation "Bowmaker to the Emperor of Japan" (retired).

In 1980, by the invitation of The Venerable Chogyam Trungpa Rinpoche, a Tibetan meditation master, and founder of Shambhala International and Naropa University, Kanjuro Shibata XX came to the United States from Japan to teach Kyudo and together with Trungpa, founded Ryuko Kyudojo (Dragon-Tiger Kyudo Practice Hall) in Boulder, Colorado. Since then Shibata Sensei has traveled extensively and established Kyudojos throughout North America and Europe. In 1985 he established permanent residence in Boulder, Colorado.

Born in Kyoto, Japan in 1921, Shibata began his Kyudo training in the Heki Ryu Bishu Chikurin-ha School of Kyudo at the age of eight. At a young age he also began training in bowmaking with his grandfather, Kanjuro Shibata XIX, in the family workshop. In 1959, upon the death of Kanjuro XIX, he officially became Kanjuro Shibata XX and assumed the duties of Imperial Bowmaker. For many years he was the master of Taiyusha Kyudojo in Kyoto, which was founded by the 18th Kanjuro Shibata in 1883.

Grandmaster Nonoy Gallano

Throughout his childhood in the Phillipines Grandmaster Nonoy Gallano studied Kali with a nearby relative. In his late teens he embarked on a 20-year quest to learn Kali from the finest Kali-Eskrimadors of his native Philippine Islands. At the end of his journey he moved to Toronto, Canada and founded the Classical Combat Eskrima Kali Association (CCEKA).

The CCEKA is dedicated to teaching the Filipino martial art, popularly known as Eskrima or Arnis. Specifically, member schools teach the Trankada-Aldabon Combat Eskrima-Kali System. Under Grandmaster Gallano's excellent tutelage and leadership, the CCEKA has been able to bring his art and style to hundreds of students throughout North America and the world.

Forward

"A true warrior looks to the future, but does not discard what he gained from the past, living each moment in the present"
- *Sensei* Kensho Furuya

The world in which we live is changing very quickly. Chances are, if you have children or grandchildren, you are often baffled at what a different world they are growing up in compared to when you were their age. This rapidly changing world is rapidly stressing us out and the research shows that people everywhere are desperately seeking balance between the best that technology and advancement offers and a life that is meaningful and fulfilling; one which encourages us to engage in community, build sustainable relationships, and reach both within and beyond ourselves. For centuries, the martial arts have provided countless individuals that exact harmony. But even this world is changing too fast for many of us to cope. Medals and championships, gold-laden belts and celebrity status has taken over much of this culture that long ago, aimed at nothing more than personal protection and self-improvement. In our quest for something meaningful; in our perpetual preference for the new and exciting, we have, to some extent, torn our connection to tradition and tainted our practice. Art has become sport.

For many years, my teacher, Master Pearson has sought to restore the balance between tradition and innovation. He has built his martial arts life on the foundation of honoring the past whilst looking ahead to the future and he has inspired his students to approach their practice with this same attitude. The articles in this book are, in many ways, a compilation of this philosophy. These are the stories, the lessons, the values, and the teachings that I have been privileged to learn at Master Pearson's feet (sometimes literally!) for over twenty years and it brings me great joy to know that they will provide inspiration and guidance to many others as well.

Master Dena Shaffer

Introduction

Years ago, four Taekwondo black belts approached me with an unusual request. The spokesperson for the group, Master Dena Shaffer (see Forward), explained that she had been reading up on the uchi-deshi (live-in) style of martial arts training found in Japan and to put it simply, they wanted to enter into a similar type program with me. Having studied a number of traditional Japanese martial arts, I was very familiar with that style of training. Immediately, I started imagining the four of them living in my house, cleaning my house, cooking for me and working outside, all while wearing their uniform style work clothing. What would the neighbors think? I could just imagine the media headlines: "Local man turns home into cult." In all seriousness, at that point in my life the lease on my Taekwondo school was up and my landlord would not let me renew. Where would they live until I found another location for my school? What about their jobs? Their families? It was immediately apparent that a traditional uchi-deshi program was out of the question for both myself and them. So instead I developed a part-time "live-in" program that would both satisfy their desire to learn traditionally and accommodate our very practical concerns.

The program consisted of my students living on the training floor, in my home, one weekend every month. During those weekends they follow a very strict uchi-deshi style of training; they get up before dawn for morning meditation, attend classes throughout the day, participate in work periods, which includes both cooking and cleaning, and finally go to bed late at night after our evening lecture. Between the training weekends, they are given homework to complete in order to continue their learning experience. Part of that homework includes the requirement to continue attending their normal Taekwondo classes and I also ask each of them to contribute weekly to our blog that one of my "inside students" had started (www.insidetaekwondo.com). The blog has been a tremendous success and has provided my students with the opportunity to share with the world their experiences and perspectives on this rare, traditional style of martial arts practice.

I have always held the belief that an instructor should never ask a student do something that they themselves would not be willing to do. Therefore, I decided that I would also complete this online requirement alongside my students. Perhaps both they and others would benefit from my sharing my own insights and thoughts when it comes to martial arts practice. This book is a small collection of a number of those posts and other articles I have written over the years and if it is well received, I have every intention of publishing several more in the future.

Agree with what I say,
Disagree agree with what I say,
Love this book,
Hate this book,
I do not care, as long as it gives you, "Something to think about…."

Contents

Philosophy — 1
There are no secrets in martial arts, only undiscovered truths. — 3
Again - There are No Secrets — 7
Demonstrations? Why do them? — 11
EGO — 13
Instructor, Student and Respect — 17
How we are Perceived as Martial Artists — 19
The Teacher and Student Relationship within Martial Arts — 23

Meditation — 27
What is Meditation? — 29
What do I Look at? or Where to Look when Meditating? — 33
The Mental Component of Reaction Time — 37
The Land of the Living Dead — 39
Meditation Analogies — 43

Mind — 47
Mu Sim (무심) – No Mind — 49
Cho Sim (초심) — 51
Bu Dong Sim (부동심) — 53
Jan Sim (잔심) — 55
Su Pa I (수파이) — 57
Dokcham — 59
Dukcham (My First Experience) — 63
Jumu – To Work & Serve — 65
What is a Kihap? — 67
Sim Sin Dan Yeon – Jeong Sin Su Yang — 71
A Fundamental Flaw in the Trigrams — 77

Body — 83
Five Direction Open Palm Set — 85
Footwork Patterns — 89
Beginning Qi (Chi) Training — 93
Breathing — 97
The Boards — 101

Culture — 105
Natto	107
Umeboshi	113
The Best Way to Get Rid of Pain after a Martial Art Class	117

Self — 119
Time Management – Why would anyone want to live like that?	121
Always seek Perfection or become Normal	125
Get out of Your Rut and Slow Down Time	129
There are a lot of Different Types of People in this World	131
Worry – Who Needs It?	137
How to Manage Your Time	141

Doctrine — 145
The 8 Defilements	147
Guidelines for Physical Development for Martial Artists	149
The Doctrine of Behavior	155

Taekwondo — 159
Taekwondo is more than just Kicking and Punching	161
The Partial Art of Taekwondo	167
Who Wants to Learn Magic?	171
The Martial Artist "Type"	173
I accept it with an Open Heart	177

Others — 179
My First Taekwondo Winter Retreat	181
Affirming Faith in Mind – Translation by Ormond McGill	187
The Best Martial Art Quotes	191
If you don't have time to do it right…	195
Get Rid of the Clocks in your Bedroom	197
8 Quick Tips	199
Meeting a Master of the Way on the Way	205

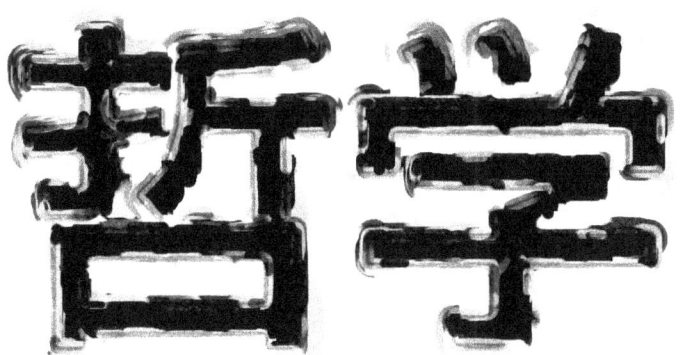

哲学

Philosophy

There are no secrets in martial arts, only undiscovered truths.

How many times have I said this? A lot. If you asked any of my black belts, I'm sure you would get a witty response, because I usually get a "Seriously? Again?" look from them whenever I utter that sentence. Back in the late 80′s and early 90′s I use to travel up to Toronto, Canada at least 3 times a month, sometimes more, to take Kali Classes. It takes 3 hours to drive from Rochester to Toronto and sometimes, depending on the border crossing, a lot longer. When I would finally arrive at the karate school, in Chinatown, that the classes were offered in, my Kali instructor Grandmaster Nonoy Gallano would inevitably introduce me to the class. I was always at a loss as to why he did this. True, I didn't attend class every week but I was in class a few times a month. It should also be noted that classes lasted an entire day, not just an hour or two. In other words, I knew all the regular students and they knew me. After the introduction, he would predictably tell me to run down the street and get him a coffee. So, after sitting in a car for 3 hours, I was running (I walked once and paid for it. I guess cold coffee is no good) 3 blocks to get a HOT coffee. After the second or third time I fetched HOT coffee, I jokingly said to Grandmaster Gallano, "You owe me a secret technique for this." After a month or so, even he would joke and offer "secret technique credit" for various things he wanted or chores he wanted me to do for him. Needless to say, he was in debt within a very short period of time.

Side Note: As far as I was concerned, this was just a joke and I would have done everything he had asked with an open heart and without complaint. I never intended to collect the "secrets".

One day, I was in Grandmaster Gallano's apartment for a private lesson and he was hungry. He wanted McDonalds (his favorite fast food restaurant was Popeyes but alas there wasn't one nearby), so off we went across the street. After I brought him his food and we sat down, I reminded him of how many "secret techniques" he owed me (it was over 50 at that point). I thought if I were lucky, it would start a conversation that I would frantically add to one of my journals that evening. Or at least, it would generate a strike that I would diligently observe in order to glean some new aspect of how to hit someone across a table. Instead, he said, "Get a knife." To which my reply was, "here?" If I remember correctly, I gleaned something new about backhand strike then. Off I went, and returned with a plastic knife. Upon my return, he stood up and told me to attack him. Remember, this was in the middle of a very large and very crowded McDonalds.

I attacked, there was a massive blur and then he stopped once my knife holding wrist was firmly held in one of his hands. He then said something along the lines of, "after I show you this, we are even". He then took his free hand and slowly pressed on the back of my hand that was holding the knife. As my wrist bent, my fingers opened and my grip on the knife was loosened. He then straightened my wrist, my fingers closed, and he sat down and started eating. There I stood, everyone looking at me holding a knife, just having attacked a very unassuming short older man, with a look of utter astonishment on my face.

I know, *everyone knows that when the wrist is bent, the fingers open* but I had never thought about it in that light before. No, there was nothing revolutionary about the actual physical technique, but the concept for me took on a profound new meaning. When you are ready to learn, the lesson will present itself. From that day on, my ability to disarm a knife holding opponent has drastically improved. I "saw the light" and I've never been the same. This was a secret that was right in front of my face, which took a plastic knife and a trip to McDonalds for me to discover.

The point is, I never thought about looking for some "secret" in something as simple as bending the wrist. There are secrets all around us. NEVER STOP LOOKING FOR THEM EVEN IN PLACES THAT YOU DON'T THINK THEY EXIST, because that tends to be where they hide.

What is is not, what is not is –
if this is not yet clear to you,
you're still far from the truth.

Something to think about...

Author Demonstrating 10 Basic Elbow Strikes with Sensei Larry White
(Early 1990's)

Again - There are No Secrets

When I was trying to come up with a topic for this article, nothing came to mind. "Seek movement and there is no movement. Seek rest and no rest comes instead." That is a lesson that is not lost on me because it is driven home over and over again. So, after a substantial amount of time sitting around and not being able to come up with anything, I decided to think back over my life as a martial artist and write about something that stuck out. This is an exercise that I do frequently. I find it very interesting how I am normally presented with some event or lesson that I hadn't thought of in years or ever for that matter.

This time I was taken back to 1990. Grandmaster Ahn and I were sitting in a Chinese restaurant that was next to his school on Reading Road (Cincinnati, OH). We were eating lunch. This was a daily event for us (Monday – Friday). I cherished very one of them because I always learned something. Normally it had something to do with the fact that my manners were lacking, but every so often it was something that would shake my world.

This article is about one such lunch. We walked over and sat down just like every other day. I ordered the same lunch special that I ordered every day. I was a vegetarian at the time and there was only one thing I could eat on the "lunch special" menu: vegetarian delight. We both sat there without saying a word, just eating. Sometimes this would happen and nothing would be said the entire meal but that was not the norm. About half way through lunch, Grandmaster Ahn looked at me and said, "There are no secrets." He was referring to secrets in Taekwondo, techniques or knowledge that only a select handful of people knew. You see I have always been slightly obsessed with learning that which isn't normally taught and Grandmaster Ahn knew that all too well.

My reply didn't come right away but when it did I only managed to get out, "but..." before he repeated, "there are no secrets." I sat there for the rest of the meal trying to find the hidden meaning in what he said. There had to be something because the alternative, that there really are no secrets, was not acceptable.

I was stuck in a no win situation. On one side was "there are no secrets" and on the other side was "my instructor is lying to me." Neither could be true. So instead of trying to come to grips with what he said, I simply filed it away in the back of my head to be dealt with at a later date. The sad thing is that the answer was right in front of me and I didn't even realize it. Grandmaster Ahn had given me a Koan, a "riddle" that isn't answerable with the logical mind. However, that is what I have to do in order to finish this article.

The answer didn't come to me until years later. Grandmaster Gallano, my Kali instructor, was doing a demonstration for a group of police officers in Toronto. He was using myself and one other student as partners for the demo. Toward the end of the demo Master Gallano was defending himself against a knife attack, executed by the other student. He proceeded to disarm him and throw him on the ground, on his stomach. He then placed his big toe on the student's back and pressed. The student flailed around and couldn't get up. I'm embarrassed to say I thought the student was faking it for Master Gallano's sake. After the demo I questioned Master Gallano about the technique. I should have known better by then because questioning him usually resulted in me being in a lot of pain. Somehow I ended up on the floor with his toe pushing on my back. It didn't really hurt but for some reason I couldn't get up or out from under his toe. My body simply didn't work. I remember thinking, "I have to learn that!" and I did that night. It really isn't that hard to do. There is a pressure point on the back that when pressed generates the desired result. It doesn't work on certain body types but the ones it does work on it is really easy to do. I could teach it to a beginner without any difficulty.

Again years went by and I was teaching a Taekwondo black belt class. I had just thrown a student on the ground that was trying to resist a joint lock I was performing for the class. I then placed my toe on the student's back and pressed. The desired effect was achieved and the student couldn't get up. I never thought twice about what I had just done. To me it was no different than doing a front kick for the class. I continued teaching and ended class without giving it a second thought. A couple of days later I overheard two of my black belts talking about how something I did in class must be a "secret." They also spent a good amount of time discussing how they were going to go about asking me to teach it to them. I walked up to them and said, "What are the two of you talking about?"

As soon as they told me, I had more than just an answer to one question. They had solved the Koan Grandmaster Ahn had given me. The secret (the big toe technique) they were talking about wasn't a secret to me but it was to them.

So instead of me telling you there are no secrets, I'll say this instead, "There are no secrets, just undiscovered truths." Never stop looking for that which you have not discovered (I haven't). It makes your journey down the path so much more enjoyable.

Something to think about...

Grandmaster Gallano and Author (Toronto, Canada)

Demonstrations? Why do them?

One day, I went to a class at a local Aikido school. We spent the entire class learning how to correctly perform aikido demos. Specifically, how to stand so that the attacker would know what technique to attack with. It was very difficult, when being the attacker, to know exactly how the defender wanted to be attacked. For example, a defender that is slightly leaning forward with their side slightly turned wants to be grabbed on the shoulder but the same posture with the head slightly inclined means the defender wants to be attacked with a knifehand strike to the neck. Sometimes it's hard to tell what the defender wants, which causes the attack to be wrong, which in turn causes the defender to not be ready for the attack. Big mess.

Before the physical class started, we spent some time talking about why Aikido students, well at least their students, and black belts do demos. The reason shocked me and no I'm not going to talk about why they do demos. I don't think the reason is bad, just very different from ours.

Ok, so why do we do demos? First of all let's look at Kyudo (it is after all one for the arts that help form the mental aspects I teach). There are two main governing bodies for Kyudo, the one that views it as a sport/martial art, that has ranks and competitions, and the other one,

Zenko, that is run by Shibata Sensei XX (my instructor). Sensei teaches a Kyudo that is practiced solely for the improvement of one's mind. There are no ranks and no competitions to inflate the students' egos. Only practice. When we shoot at the target, the thought of "I hit" or "I didn't hit" the target never enters our minds. Instead, the arrow and the target simply reflect the true nature of our shooting back at us. This reflection becomes our instructor, and sometimes it is a very critical instructor. Over time the target fades and there is no distinction between the target and the kyudoka (archer). Think of it this way, your arm is your arm but it is still part of your body. Okay, back on the topic of demonstrations. I'll come back to the target in another article.

In Kyudo, when we shoot for a demonstration we are revealing our true nature to the people that are watching. All of our flaws and imperfections are presented for all to see. It is how we, as the students doing the demo, conduct ourselves while faced with these flaws, that is the true beauty (or ugliness) of the demo. Imagine a student that is shooting for a group of people. As the student raises the Yumi (bow) to shoot, and he drops the arrow. There are two ways the student could deal with this. He could protect his ego by starting over or even have a small temper tantrum and get upset at either himself or his equipment. After all, there has to be something wrong with the arrow or it would never have been dropped. On the other hand, he can continue on with the shooting, never breaking his form (as if the arrow falling was suppose to have happened), and finish with no expression of emotion. This is a true demonstration of a martial artist. None of us are perfect and that imperfection will come out during a demo. It is how we, as the student doing the demo, handle this imperfection that demonstrates our martial art.

This approach is exactly the reason for why my school does a demonstration. It is a learning experience for the student. The demo, like the target, reflects all of our imperfections back at us in crystal clarity. Anyone can break a stack of bricks, however not everyone can remain calm and in complete control when they don't all break.

Something to think about...

EGO

Last week, I took a class at a local martial art school. I have been taking classes there on and off (more off than on) for the past 20 years. Even though the underlying technique of the motions covered sometimes directly contradicts what I teach in Taekwondo, I toughly enjoy going to classes because it allows me to be a color belt again. Yes you heard it correctly, I have been going there for 20 years and I am a color belt (remember the off part is longer than the on part). Anyway, back to the class. We had just finished warm-ups and stretches when the instructor broke the students up into two groups. There were 6 students in class that night, which meant 3 students per group. I was in a group with one black belt and one color belt (the same rank as me). The instructor then demonstrated an application of a standard wrist lock. Basically what happened next was one at a time both of us color belts would grab the black belt and she would defend herself with the technique. Then the other color belt would bow to her and replace her as the person that was being attacked (grabbed). Then I would grab him, then the black belt would grab and then I'd bow and replace him. Then it was my turn. This process would happen over and over again until the instructor introduced a different technique.

> **I LOVE MYSELF**

Everything was going just great until the instructor introduced the third technique. After he demonstrated it, the black belt was up and the other student grabbed her. She couldn't do the technique. It had nothing to do with a lack of ability but because she, if I had to guess, had never done this specific defense before. You could immediately see (and feel) a shift in her mental state. She was getting very frustrated and upset. However, this new attitude wasn't directed toward herself (due to her inabilities) but rather at the instructor and the two of us. In addition, it got much much worse after the two of us were able to do the technique. Was it because we were better than the black belt? No, it's because we had the benefit of watching the instructor fix the black belt's technique after she did it wrong. Also, I had done the technique before. The rest of the class (while in that group) went downhill from there. It would be one thing if the black belt's new attitude only affected her but it didn't. Within a very short period of time, she stopped bowing to either of us when we would switch with her. Then she started slowing down the entire group by taking little breaks between techniques. Why did all this happen? Ego.

Martial art students often think the hardest part of their training is learning a specific technique, but in reality it is keeping the "ego" in check. The thought, "I'm better than the black belt is," never entered my mind and if I had to guess it never entered the other student's mind. Therefore, the black belt wasted a good portion of a class because her ego was worried about something that it didn't have to worry about. This happens all of the time in almost every martial art school. Students and black belts are more focused on how other people perceive them than they are on their own techniques. What a waste of time. If the black belt in the above mentioned class had focused on learning the technique instead of getting upset, she might actually be able to do it the next time it is taught.

Traditionally, the highest dropout rank in a martial art, other than white belt, is 1st degree black belt. Why? Because, that is when the "ego" starts really coming into play. What a waste. How many times have you seen two black belt's, that have never met, walk up to each other and immediately count the number of tips on the other's belt to determine who outranks who? What a waste. How many times have you wasted an entire class upset at yourself for not knowing something or not being able to do something someone else could do? What a waste. How many times have you seen someone doing a breaking demonstration, only to fail and have a temper tantrum? What a waste. Etc. etc. etc. etc.

I have found this to be a very difficult article to write. It's very hard to talk about this in written from especially with a wide-ranging group of readers. If I were writing for a group of Kyudo students, this would be easy because eliminating ego is a main focus of the art. In order to leave you with something other than wondering thoughts, I'll say this, notice the ego. Have you noticed how when you get a new car, you tend to see a lot more of them on the road? Once you notice your ego, you will see it pop its ugly head up all the time. That is when you can start to get the ego under control. It is a never-ending battle that will last as long as you practice martial arts. In fact it gets harder for most people as their rank gets higher. Remember you are taking Taekwondo for yourself and not to impress other people or students. Look at every failing as a learning experience. Some of my most profound insights into Taekwondo occurred when I failed at something. I hope I continue to fail, because when I stop failing my ego has won.

Something to think about...

Knife Seminar held at Ahn Taekwondo Institute (Cincinnati, Ohio)
Photos taken by Sara Kitchen

Instructor, Student and Respect

I thought I would talk a little more about respect in this article. I am away from my computer (out of the USA) and once again I find myself writing an article on my phone.

A student of mine once asked me, on the way to a non-taekwondo seminar, "what should I call you at the seminar?" Unfortunately, I cannot write what my reply was. Needless to say, I basically told him he could call me anything he wanted. Would you ever ask your instructor that? A better question might be, would or do you ever call your instructor by a different name off the training floor than when on the training floor?

Because most of you that are reading this are Taekwondo students, I'll use my Taekwondo instructor, Grandmaster Kyongwon Ahn as an example. I had the privilege of working with Grandmaster Ahn for 2 years (as national director of Dan promotions for the USTU). I spent over 60 hours a week with him. Some of that time was on the training floor but a good portion was off the training floor: business meetings, eating at restaurants (we ate almost every lunch together for 2 years), traveling, etc. Whenever I addressed him, I always called him, "Master Ahn" (he preferred it over Grandmaster Ahn at the time). It didn't matter if I was on the training floor or off the training floor; the thought of calling him anything but Master Ahn never entered my mind. I never thought, "what should I call him now that I'm not on the training floor." For those of you that are reading this that know him, would you ever think of calling him anything other than "Master Ahn?" Of course not! Why? Chances are, the level of your respect for him is so high that the thought of addressing him without his title would never enter your mind.

So, back to the initial question, what do you call your instructor off the training floor? If it is different from what you call him/her on the floor, why is that? I would suggest it has to do with your level of respect for your instructor. For those of you that are saying, "it has nothing to do with respect", you should call Grandmaster Ahn by his first name the next time you see him. I know what you are thinking; "I'll get in trouble if I do that." You will, if anyone hears you other than Grandmaster Ahn, but if it's just the two of you, I can almost guarantee he will simply act as if you did nothing wrong. It would be the same as asking him, "what should I call you at the restaurant?" He will simply make a mental note of the "event" and move on.

Respect is something that should always be monitored by both the student and the instructor. It can be used to gauge the relationship. As a student, if the level of respect you have for our instructor isn't high, move on and find one that it is high with. How can you expect to learn from someone that you don't have a high level of respect for? Oh wait I've heard this response a lot, "my level of respect for the head instructor is really high, just not my level of respect for the assistant instructor." If that is the case, only take classes from the head instructor. If that isn't possible, move on. I know this might seem harsh, but you can't hope to learn, to a high level, if that respect isn't present.

As an instructor I'm constantly monitoring the level of respect my students have toward me. Who do you think I am going to spend time teaching non-curriculum material to? It's not going to be the students that don't have respect for me. No it's not an ego thing. It's simply a fact that students that have a high level of "true" respect learn better than the ones that don't. It goes back to the article: how would you greet a master of the way, on the way?

Something to think about...

How we are Perceived as Martial Artists

Back in the early 90's I attended a 10-day martial art retreat in northern Vermont. It was a traditional Japanese martial art retreat, in that we all wore kimonos and hakama. We dressed like that the majority of the time. One day I decided that I would run and get gas for my car during my lunch break. I did not think at the time that I would remember this little outing almost 20 years later.

Before completing this story it is important to give you a little background on the area surrounding the retreat. The retreat was in the middle of nowhere. The closest McDonalds was about 20 miles away. It definitely wasn't a common occurrence to have someone walking around in a kimono.

So off I went to get gas, looking like someone right out of the Seven Samurai and not thinking anything of it. It turns out that the only gas station I could find (I ended up finding more the next year) was also the favorite hangout spot for the local teenagers and people who looked like they were in their early twenties but still thought of themselves as teenagers. I again didn't think anything of it and got out of the car and started pumping gas. You would have thought I was an alien that had just beamed down to earth and was being seen for the first time. From the time I started pumping gas until I was pulling out of the parking lot, I was bombarded with every imaginable insult. The mildest was the strange otherworldly sounds that some of them were making in an attempt to sound like, I'm assuming, Bruce Lee. It should be noted that I never really felt like the "aggression" was going to escalate to the point were they were going to physically confront me. However, it still wasn't very enjoyable, especially the, "does your mommy dress you like that?" comment. Joking aside, I was glad to get out of there.

A couple of days later, I was invited to go to lunch with the master instructor for the retreat. This was a huge honor and I immediately accepted. I went with him and two of the assistant instructors and his personal assistant. We went to eat at a local restaurant and yes we all wore our kimonos. No one really even looked twice at us (it turns out that the instructor had been going there every day of the retreat for lunch and everyone there was use to our interesting dress). After lunch it was decided that we were all going to the local mall. Truth be told, I was never asked if I wanted to go to a mall in the middle of nowhere looking like a samurai.

Off we went. Once there, I realized that the local's definition of a mall was substantially different from mine. Let's put it this way, their "mall" would fit inside one of my mall's hub stores. The driver dropped all of us off at the entrance, found a parking stop and then joined us before we all proceeded into the mall. As customary, we quickly went to hold the doors open of our instructor. He then, as was customary for him, insisted we enter first. Somehow, I was the first one to enter the mall (at the time I was the junior to everyone I was with and for some reason none of them wanted to enter first). Literally the second I walked through the door I saw them, the group of teenagers from the gas station (ok maybe it wasn't the exact same group but they looked and acted the same). As soon as they saw me the comments and the Bruce Lee sounds started. These only intensified when the other two instructors walked through the door. By the time the assistant walked through, the group was so loud that they were drowning out all the mall's background sound. Then it was as if someone pushed a mall remote's mute button. When our instructor walked through the door, all the teenagers immediately stopped making comments, noises and looked away as if they were all 5 years old and were just caught doing something they shouldn't be doing by their parents. We then walked around the mall without a side-glance or comment or noise from anyone.

It was as if everyone in the mall knew our instructor and they were all scared of him. So why does this event stick in my mind? He was and still is after all the twentieth generation head of the martial art he teaches. There is no one that even comes close to his knowledge in his art. He was like a lion walking through a herd of zebra (that can't run away).

So again, why does this event stick in my mind? Because our instructor, Kanjuro Shibata XX Sensei, was and is the twentieth generation head of the Heki Ryu Bishu Chikurin-ha school of Kyudo. For those of you that don't know, Kyudo is the "Way of the Bow." We spend all of our time learning how to shoot a bow, not how to punch or kick or how to defend ourselves. From a physical standpoint Shibata Sensei could no more defend himself in a physical conflict than any other person of his age. I can say with certainty that if one of us were to have been mugged, it would not have been Sensei. So why the attitude of every one in the mall?

Kanjuro Shibata XX Sensei

As martial artists we, as another article pointed out, wear a belt with two ends. One end represents the physical part of our art and the other end represents the mental part of our art. Most people assume that the mental part consists of memorizing terminology, the history of Taekwondo, and the various other "things" that have to be memorized. Some people even think this part contains meditation practice, breathing techniques, energy work (Chi Kung), etc. Very few people think it contains what this entire article is devoted to: our self-image. As martial artists, as we practice every day and make small but perceivable improvements, so too does our self-image improve. It isn't our perception of how we look; it is our understanding that we are capable of achieving anything. I once asked one of my instructors,

"How can you do that?" His response was, "because I know I can." When we start knowing that we can do anything, our outward expression of our self-image comes across in the form of self-confidence, indomitable spirit, and sometimes even arrogance (like any journey in life it is possible to go down the wrong path and in this case it would be an instructor with a huge EGO).

Start watching our seniors and take note of how you perceive them and how other people perceive them. You can easily tell how far along an instructor is in their training simple by observing their self-image.

Something to think about...

Kanjuro Shibata XX Sensei
(Boulder, Colorado)

The Teacher and Student Relationship within Martial Arts

In this article I'd like to talk about the teacher and student relationship within martial arts. This relationship is very misunderstood by non-martial artists and even by a lot of students and instructors. Let me make this really simple. As an instructor it is my job to transfer my knowledge to my students in the most efficient and safe way possible. That's it. It's the students' job to learn the material as completely and safely as possible. That's it.

So why is this relationship so different from that of say a high school teacher and his student, or a soccer coach and his player, or a parent and his child? The roots of this can be traced to the material that is being taught. Martial arts are potentially dangerous to practice and the knowledge the students gain can be used, even if not intentionally, to seriously hurt another person. It is therefore very important that a student, without question, follows their instructor's commands and follows them immediately. If the student doesn't, he/she or their partner could end up seriously injured. Imagine, if you will, two students are practicing a newly learned combination and in the process of executing one of the motions it is apparent to the instructor that it is being done incorrectly. The instructor immediately tells the students to stop. If the correct relationship exists between the instructor and his students, they will both immediately stop without question. If that relationship doesn't exist one or both of the students might have continued the combination and then not seeing the potential danger, one or more of the students could have gotten seriously injured.

I have said numerous times to my students that if one of my instructors asked me to jump off a bridge I would without hesitation and absolutely without any fear. How is that possible? Why would I be willing to throw myself off a bridge? I love BASE-jumping of course. No, joking aside, the reason is, I completely trust my instructors. I know that none of them would ever ask me to do anything that would seriously injure me. That's why I would jump off the bridge with no fear, because I know, without question, that I wouldn't get hurt by jumping. How is that possible? How can I not get hurt? I have no idea, but somehow I would be safe.

I have learned martial arts from a lot of people, which in no way makes them all my instructors. I am very selective as to the people I consider my instructors. I don't use that title lightly, because after all I'm willing to do anything they asked of me. After almost 40 years of taking martial arts there are only 4 individuals I consider my instructors (and one of them isn't even a martial artist anymore). I have been very lucky to have learned from a large group of very talented individuals but other than those 4, none of them made the transition in my mind to "instructor." So what causes an individual to make this transition? A lot of factors: how they interact with other instructors, with students, their ability to teach, their ability to do the techniques themselves or at least demonstrate a good mental understanding of how the techniques should be performed, how they act outside of the school, etc, etc, etc. The list just goes on and on and on.

Over 15 years ago I came up with one unifying factor that takes all of those other factors into account. I call it the "float" factor (its how far they float off the ground in my mind). Every time someone I'm learning from does something positive, his or her float factor increases. Every time they do something negative, their float factor decreases. Some of the instructor's actions can easily be assigned into one of these two groups, however for the most part it is up to the individual student to assign the action to the group. These ups and downs are not equal. For me, it takes four or five positives to equal one negative, and that's only for a small negative, because in my mind a "large" negative is unacceptable and I would stop learning from anyone that had one of those.

So how does someone who is teaching me become my "instructor?" They always have to be "floating." There is never an excuse for any true martial art instructor not to be. I realize that even a great instructor will have some negatives but the positives will drastically outnumber them. From the day I met them, all four of my "instructors" have never not floated.

A little over ten years ago I was having this discussion with a group of my black belts. They all insisted that I "floated" for all of them and therefore implied that they would "jump off a bridge" for me if I asked them to. Believe me, I have no delusions that I "float" for all my students. In fact, knowing fist hand of all my flaws, I'd be surprised if I really "float" of any of my students. I told them all this and they very politely told me that I was crazy. So I sent them all into a room off the training floor and closed the door. I told them to wait and that I would return momentarily. A couple of minutes later I returned with a rope and a blindfold. I told the black belts that I was going to test each of them to see whether or not I truly "float" for them. I then proceeded to blindfold one of them and tie his hands behind his back. The black belt was then led out onto the training floor. My school's floor, at that time, was carpet on top of cement (in other words – very hard). I told him that he had to fall forward onto the ground from a standing position and that he could not bend his knees. He was told that if he bent his knees, and they touched the ground before his chest hit the floor, he failed. He was faced with the "jumping off the bridge" situation. To this black belt's mind, it was impossible for him not to get hurt; he just had to trust me. To make things worse, I continued to talk to him from a point to his rear, so that he knew that I wasn't going to catch him.

Unbeknownst to the black belts I had moved a pile of very soft mats (thicker and softer than a mattress) onto the training floor before I brought the first one of them out. One at a time I would bring them out and position each of them in front of this stack before I told them what to do. So there was no way they would get hurt when they fell. I had expected some of them to pass and some of them to fail and my expectations were correct. I didn't do the test to inflate or deflate my ego; I did it for my black belts. Until you are placed in that "no win" situation you truly don't know how you would react. Some of the black bets simply sat there in disbelief not understanding how they could have failed and some sat there is disbelief not understanding how they could have passed. Each and every one of them learned something about themselves that day.

So, would you pass this test if your instructor gave it to you? If you answer "no", its time to ask yourself, "why wouldn't I." Your answer should provide you with:

Something to think about...

Author Executing Various Stabs & Hooks
(Early 1990's)

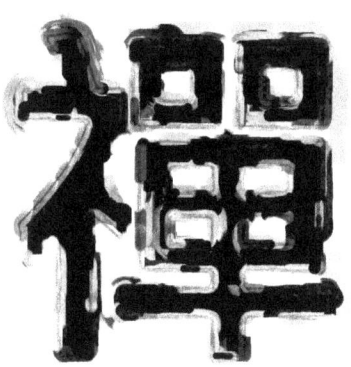

Meditation

What is Meditation?

I'm currently finishing up my newest book, "Do Meditation". Other than a ton of pictures having to be taken, the book, for the most part, is finished. Recently, I have been thinking a lot about meditation, partially because I have been finishing the book, but also because I have given a few talks covering the subject. Therefore, I thought "meditation" would be a great topic for this week's article.

As a statistics professor, I frequently get looks of disgust when I tell people I teach Statistics. These looks are normally accompanied by, "yuck!" or "I hated statistics!" For the life of me I don't understand their reactions. Is there a big conspiracy of Stats professors, that I'm not part of, that intentionally makes an exciting subject the anchor for such responses? My classes are very exciting. We, the students and I, have coordination, reflex and head stand competitions during classes. I bring in arrows, atlatls, wolf traps (that I stick my hand in) and various wilderness survival tools. I do magic tricks, I sometimes do a stage hypnosis show and I teach all the students body language to tell what someone is really thinking. I could go on and on but needless to say the students that leave my class at the end of the semester say, "I loved my stats class" when asked (well, the ones that pass do anyway).

Why? My class covers the same material that everyone who hates statistics took. Believe me when I say this, I'm not some sort of great statistics teacher. Most of the professors I learned stats from are vastly more knowledgeable than I am in statistics and have a lot more teaching experience. The reason they don't hate stats and in a lot of cases love it, is because I hide it (statistics) in fun.

> *Figures often beguile me, particularly when*
> *I have the arranging of them myself;*
> *in which case the remark attributed to Disraeli*
> *would often apply with justice and force:*
> "There are three kinds of lies: lies, damned lies, and statistics."
> Mark Twain

So back to the topic of the article, "What is meditation?" When asked, most people conjure up images of a bald person, with robes, sitting in a very uncomfortable position and gazing at a wall for hours on end. I find that I get similar responses when people find out I meditate every day as I do from people when I tell them I teach statistics. "I hate meditating!" "I'd rather get teeth pulled".

Meditation does not have to be painful or boring. I'll say it again. **Meditation does not have to be painful or boring**. It is true that for a large percentage of the population, seated meditation isn't their idea of fun but here is kicker, you don't have to sit in front of a wall and/or be in pain to meditate. You can hide it in "fun"! So what is meditation?

When we as humans go about our daily lives, our brains exist in a specific state. If we "hooked" someone, in this state, up to an Electroencephalograph, it would show that the person's brain is producing "beta" waves. These waves are all over the place. Think of a 5-year-old boy after consuming a couple sodas and a bag of candy.

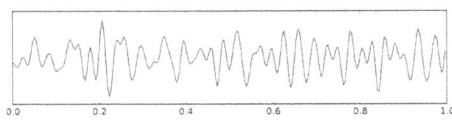
Beta Waves

So what is "Meditation"? It is ANY practice that moves or forces our minds out of "beta" waves and into "alpha" waves (or Theta or Delta). "Alpha" waves are smooth up and down waves. Think of your grandmother rocking back and forth in a rocking chair. This is the realm of meditation and it is easier to get into than you might think. In addition, just like everything else you do multiple times in life, it gets easier and faster to make the switch with each repetition.

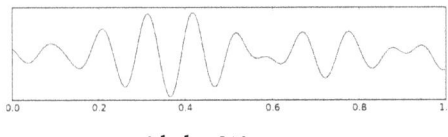
Alpha Waves

So how do we make this switch? Sitting in front of a wall will do the trick but why not go for a walk through the woods or enjoy a freshly cooked dinner or fold a fish out of paper. In the beginning, any practice that slows us down and allows us to be mindful of what we are doing can be used to make the "switch." Back in the 90's I attended a wilderness survival class. The instructor was teaching a class on Apache (a Native American Tribe from the Southwest) philosophy. He had a very very old Buffalo hide with a drawing of four nested circles on it. This drawing was used by Apache Shamans to explain the different "states" of mind an individual could dwell in. It was made over 200 years before the Electroencephalograph was even invented. It is proof that they were aware of Beta, Alpha, Theta and Delta waves, even if they didn't call them that, before the first car was even made. The reason I bring this up is that they called the "beta wave state", the "Land of the Living Dead." They wanted to minimize the amount of time they spent in this "land" and they constantly strived to live their lives in the "alpha realm". One tool they used for this is something I now cover in every Meditation class I teach. Their term for this loosely translates into, "wide-angle vision". Basically, it is one of the simplest ways to make the switch: walk slowly and focus on your peripheral vision.

So I guess the question then becomes, "Why Meditate?" The answer to that question could be an article in itself. For me, the main reason I meditate is to eliminate or substantially reduce random thoughts. When I eat an orange, I want to eat an orange, not think about bills or what I'm going to be eating for dinner tomorrow. It is truly amazing how good an orange tastes when you "just eat" one. It really amazes me when someone I know tells me how much they love to eat a certain food and when they actually eat it, they talk about all sorts of random stuff and don't enjoy what they are eating.

Have you ever been in a conversation with someone and you can tell they are not even listening to you? They are off in some mental world that is definitely not the one your conversation exists in. Can you imagine how much better everyone would actually communicate if people "just talked" to the person they were talking to? How many car accidents would we have if people "just drove"? How much better would a high school student's grades be if he/she "just took exams"? How much faster could I "just write this article" if my mind didn't keep wondering to the fact that I didn't get any sleep last night? You get my point. The more you meditate the fewer random thoughts you will have.

Something to think about...

Image/Photo Citations

Image 1:   EEG Beta – Hugo Gamboa – 11/01/2012
http://en.wikipedia.org/w/index.php?title=File:Eeg_beta.svg

Image 2:   EEG Alpha – Hugo Gamboa – 11/01/2012
http://en.wikipedia.org/w/index.php?title=File:Eeg_alpha.svg

What do I Look at? or Where to Look when Meditating?

This article was taken from my book "Do Meditation". In the beginning of the book there are several chapters on the basics of meditation: "How do I Sit", "How do I Breathe", and

What do I Look at? Aka. What do I See?

When I first started meditating, there was really nothing that bothered me more than the answers I would receive from my instructors when I would ask them, "What do I look at?" Their answers would inevitably be some nonsense (at least I thought it was nonsense at the time) like "nothing" or "just let your eyes defocus". The problem was that all the initial styles of meditation I practiced had me facing a wall and the ones that didn't, had me facing the back of someone else meditating. So my thinking was, "how can I not look at something that is right in front of my face and, in the case of a wall, takes up my entire field of vision?"

I was a very determined young meditator, so I was determined to NOT look at the wall, NOT to look at the person's back in front of me, NOT to see all the interesting patterns in the texture of the wall, NOT to wonder if the person's clothing had ever been washed because they didn't look like they had, NOT to wonder if there was some mystical meaning in the choice of the wall color, NOT to get upset at the person in front of me moving ever so slightly and most importantly, NOT to think about NOT looking at anything. "Looking" back over all the time I wasted actually not not looking, I think why couldn't someone have simply told me what took me years to learn and what could have been summed up in one sentence. I think of how much further I'd be along in my practice today if they had. I think, "Ahhhhhhhhhhhhhhhhh"

Slightly over ten years after I started actively meditating, a good friend of mine gave me a book written by his wilderness survival instructor. I had grown up in a small town in upstate New York, spent most of my childhood playing in the woods, and he therefore thought I might like the book. Not only did I like it, I loved it. Immediately after finishing the book I signed up for a wilderness survival class taught by the book's author. The "standard class", as it was called, was broken up into three major sections: survival, tracking and philosophy. I immensely enjoyed the entire class, but boy was I upset when the instructor taught all the students in the class a technique called, "wide-angle vision". He told everyone by simply allowing their eyes to "focus" on items in the peripheral field of vision, instead of what was in front of them, their minds would naturally shift into a meditative state. In other words, out of beta waves and into alpha waves. Then he told us all to go outside, slowly walk around and practice "wide-angle vision". So off the class went. I thought, "This is going to be a disaster." I figured that everyone would go out, walk around for at most a few minutes and then go off and do other things until the class was called back. This is a typical response to a beginner's first exposure to a meditative practice. The reason for this is that most beginners, when exposed to their thinking minds, are overwhelmed by how much they are actually thinking. These "random" thoughts are normally overlooked and ignored, liked background noise in a public mall, but when they focus their conscious mind's spotlight on them, they become overwhelmed and give up. However, that wasn't what happened, not at all. Instead, everyone started walking around, and within a few minutes, they all slowed down and you could almost feel a shift in the group's consciousness. Not a single student, out of the approximately 100 students that were there, stopped until they were called back. As for my experience, and why I was upset, I immediately noticed my mind shifting out of beta waves. I almost feel over, I was so stunned. How is it that something so simple can be so effective? It worked. It was easy. Anyone could do it with no experience or practice. "This is totally not fair. They should all have to go through what I went through," is all I kept thinking. After time passed however, I realized how much this simple technique could benefit all my meditation students. Instead of telling them what I had been told, "defocus your eyes," I could give them a simple technique that would actually help their meditation practice.

So, "What do I Look at?" and "What should you look at?" Nothing. Just let your eyes defocus. In other words, don't focus on what is in front of you, focus on what is not in front of you and eventually you will be focusing on nothing at all (and a lot faster than I did, due to the fact that you know this simple technique). You will be solely working on your meditation, everything else will drop away and you will truly be "looking at nothing!!"

Something to think about...

Author Executing a Go Cho Form
(Early 1990's)

The Mental Component of Reaction Time

Currently I'm down in Key West, Florida and I don't have access to a computer to write this article. Therefore, due to the time required to write a short article on a phone, this article will be shorter than I would like. Reaction time, in the case of martial arts, is the time it takes from the instant a technique is executed by an opponent until the counter technique (block or strike) has been fully executed. Total reaction time is made up of two parts: mental reaction time and physical reaction time. Mental reaction time is the amount of time between the instant the opponent executes a technique and the moment our physical response starts. Physical reaction time is the amount of time between the instant the physical response starts and the moment the physical technique has been fully executed. Most martial artists are constantly striving to reduce their total reaction time by shortening their physical reaction time. There are a lot of practices that are commonly taught in typical classes that will also help reduce physical reaction time. Instructors typically do this by having student work on individual techniques to make them faster and more efficient and some of them even have students work on executing the technique in a more relaxed state. Both of these practices will reduce physical reaction time.

What I would like to focus on in this article is the mental reaction time. What happens during this phase of the reaction is: your subconscious perceives a technique that has been executed by your opponent. This information then passes on to the conscious mind (the thinking mind). Then the thinking mind needs to decide what to do. Once all the possibilities have been weighed and a decision has been made, the command to move is then sent out to the muscular system of the body. So how do you improve (shorten) this time? There are two primary ways. The first way is to practice the counter for a technique over and over again. For example, if you always practice the same counter to a knife hand strike, over and over and over your subconscious will respond to the technique (stimulus) without passing it on to the conscious mind. This only works when there is only one response to the technique and it has been practiced extensively. The problem is that sometimes the practiced response might not be the best technique for the counter. However, the mental response time is substantially reduced if the conscious mind step is eliminated.

The other way of shortening the response time is simply to meditate. The more someone meditates the easier it is for that person to switch their mind out of beta waves and into alpha waves. Once that has been achieved, response time is substantially reduced and unlike the previous method, this allows for the mind to pick an appropriate response to the technique. In other words, if you want to decrease the mental component of your response time, meditate!

Something to think about...

The Land of the Living Dead and How I Can Escape by Understanding Brainwaves

I am constantly asked by my black belts, "Why do we do that?" The "that" they are referring to might be the constantly changing time we, as a class, sit before we bow every class. It might be "that" we are folding paper into fish and not kicking or it might be "that" we are staring at a wall for prolonged periods of time.

Note: The next paragraph describes a very **ABRIDGED** version of how my classes are opened.

Lets take a look at the first example concerning the bowing in process before class. In my schools we bow into class by lining up in straight line. Unlike a lot of Taekwondo Schools, everyone lines up in the same line. The instructor stands in front of the line and faces the students. Once everyone is lined up correctly, everyone sits after the instructor sits. Then there is a period of sitting that takes place. The length of this period is up to the instructor.

This period of sitting is what I receive a lot of questions concerning. You see, the length always changes and it never seems to follow a pattern. So why does it change and why do we do it at all?

A large number of martial art schools have their students sit for a minute or two before classes start, as a form of meditative practice. Unfortunately, for a large number of these students there will be little to no benefit from this practice and therefore the practice is a waste of time for them. So why do we and so many other schools continue to have everyone sit before class? This might sound selfish, but for the benefit of the instructor.

As humans, our brains function on 4 general levels (in my schools we call these levels, realms). In modern times these levels have been classified by using an Electroencephalograph (EEG). The EEG monitors brain waves and each of the four levels displays a different "wave" on the EEG. Make no mistake, the ancient cultures knew of the existence of these same exact levels, even before anyone even knew that brain waves existed. Below is a list of the four brain waves that correspond to the four general functional levels:

Beta Waves

Name: The Realm of Men
Characteristics: Minimal body control, mental power, physical ability and awareness.

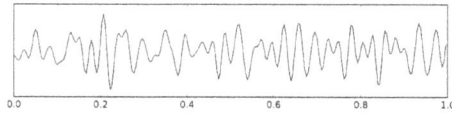

Alpha Waves

Name: The Realm of Warriors
Characteristics: Good body control, heightened mental power, heightened physical ability and good awareness.

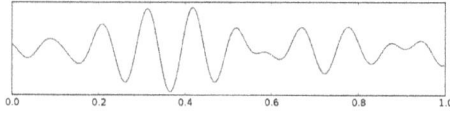

Theta Waves

Name: The Realm of the Masters
Characteristics: Excellent body control, insightful mental power and excellent awareness.

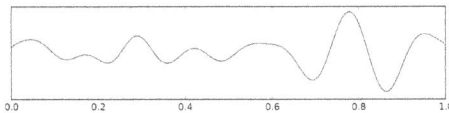

Delta Waves

Name: The Realm of the Spirits
Characteristics: Control of automatic body functions.

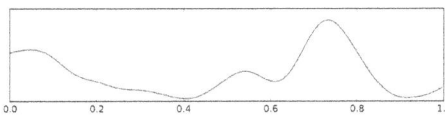

When most people go about their daily lives they live/function in beta waves. The Apache called this realm, "The land of the living dead." When an individual is in this realm, their mental and physical abilities are at their lowest possible level. Their awareness of their surroundings is extremely low and their ability to control their bodies is diminished. When our brain waves slow down some, we enter the "Realm of Warriors", in other words: alpha waves. This is what athletes refer to as "being in the zone." Everything is heightened: mental power, physical ability, awareness and body control. We have better reflexes, we can memorize things faster, we have better coordination/balance, we perceive time passage slower, etc. This is where a martial artist wants to be when practicing, if not all the time.

Just like anything that is practiced over and over again, the time required to execute a technique or in this case to switch brain waves from beta to alpha gets shorter and shorter. A beginner might require 15 – 20 minutes of a meditative practice to make the switch. However, most instructors, that have been practicing martial arts for most of their lives, can usually make this switch on command, or very quickly. So the pause before bowing is for the instructor to make this switch. That is what determines the length of the pause.

The other two "why" questions mentioned at the beginning of this article are also related to brain waves. Both doing origami and doing seated meditation will cause the brain to switch into alpha waves if performed for a sufficient length of time. And remember, the more times your brain makes the switch, the faster it will make it.

Therefore, the next time you think to yourself, "Why do we do that?" Ask yourself this, "Is it to change brain waves?"

Something to think about...

Image/Photo Citations

Image 1:   EEG Beta – Hugo Gamboa – 11/01/2012
           http://en.wikipedia.org/w/index.php?title=File:Eeg_beta.svg

Image 2:   EEG Alpha – Hugo Gamboa – 11/01/2012
           http://en.wikipedia.org/w/index.php?title=File:Eeg_alpha.svg

Image 3:   EEG Theta – Hugo Gamboa – 11/01/2012
           http://en.wikipedia.org/w/index.php?title=File:Eeg_theta.svg

Image 4:   EEG Delta – Hugo Gamboa – 11/01/2012
           http://en.wikipedia.org/w/index.php?title=File:Eeg_delta.svg

Meditation Analogies

Having done meditation in one form or another for most of my life, I have come across lots of analogies concerning it. The most common of these being, "the reflection of the moon." In this analogy the clarity of a meditation practitioner's mind is likened to the clarity of the reflection of the moon on a puddle of water.

When someone begins to meditate for the first time, their mind runs wild with lots of random thoughts. It is very difficult, if not impossible, for the beginner to clear his/her mind. In the moon analogy, the moon barely looks like a white circle on the surface of the water, due to the choppiness and muddiness of the water caused by the constant wind. As the meditator continues with his/her training, the random thoughts tend to lesson.

Over time there might be large gaps with no random thoughts. The moon is now visible as a moon in the reflection. The wind has stopped, except for an occasional gust, the surface of the water is flattening out and the dirt is starting to settle. Sometimes the moon can even be seen in perfect clarity as if it was being observed directly. Otherwise, the wind kicks up some small waves on the water and causes the reflection to distort. The wind is short lived however, and the water calms down again. This dance of wind and no wind plays out randomly as do the thoughts of the meditator.

After years of practice, the water is crystal clear and so is the reflection of the moon. One would be hard pressed to tell if they were looking directly at the moon or at a reflection of it. At this point the meditator sits with no random thoughts for extremely long periods of time.

The second most common analogy is, "the pine tree through the window." This analogy starts with the beginner looking through a frost-covered window at a pine tree. Initially, all he/she can see is a green shape in a rough form of a triangle, due to the frost on he window and the bad winter storm outside. As the frost starts to melt and the storm subsides, the experienced meditator can finally start to see the pine tree. Once all the frost has disappeared the master meditator can see the tree in all of its beauty. All the minute details are visible: the individual pine needles, the pinecones and even the true texture of the bark.

My favorite analogy wasn't presented to me in a long story or even in some Hollywood like mystical setting, as the other two were. I was simply sitting and waiting for one of my instructors to speak after a round of meditation. When, after expecting a 30-minute talk on meditation, he came into the room and simply said, "Dust Happens!" and then left, I was very surprised. At first I thought, "That's it?" But, over the years I have developed a strong love (and sometimes hate) for those two words. Think about it for a moment, "Dust Happens!" No matter what you do, you will have dust. You can clean a room for hours and hours until every surface is dust free. If you leave for a few days and come back, even if no one goes into the room when you are gone, there will be dust. There will be even more dust if the room is used for those few days you are gone.

So what is one to do? The only thing that can be done: clean on a daily basis. We can even purchase equipment to make the cleaning faster and more efficient, but if you want to keep up with the dust you must clean daily. You can probably guess how this relates to meditation. The beginner enters a room that hasn't been cleaned in years and starts cleaning. The problem is that because there is so much dust/dirt the very act of cleaning stirs up lots of dust into the air and it will simply settle someplace else a few moments later. After lots and lots and lots of cleaning, the room is finally clean. However, taking a break now would definitely be a mistake, because when you finally returned to cleaning, the room would be dirty again. Granted it wouldn't be as dirty as in the beginning, but it would be a lot dirtier and take a lot longer to clean then if a little time had been spent cleaning on a daily basis.

So the advantages of cleaning daily include the small amount of dirt and the short time required to clean it. The same is true for meditation, once the mind has been disciplined daily practice is essential. It is much better to practice daily for a short period of time than to practice weekly for a long period of time.

Something to think about...

There is a lot of Dust out there!

Mind

Mu Sim (무심) – No Mind
(Without Mind)

In this article I am going to talk about one of the Four Minds of a Martial Artist. As I sit down to write this my mind drifts off to the trip to Maine I am about to undertake. I apologize in advance for the quality of the article. My mind is elsewhere (is it?).

"Mu" comes from the Chinese word "Wu" (無) which means: negative, no or not. 無 contains the radical 火. The character "火" means fire or burn. "Sim" comes from the Chinese word "Shin" (心) which in this case means: mind. Therefore, Mu Sim means "No Mind" or "The Mind that burns away thoughts." When a martial artist enters this state of mind they are free of fear, anger, ego and all forms of thinking. They exist in the moment and subconsciously react to stimulus.

Mu Sim not only benefits martial artists on a mental level, it also benefits them on a physical level. Thinking mind is very slow to react, where as Mu Sim reacts instantly. Typically, a student enters Mu Sim for the first time while sparring or while executing a form during a promotion exam. If asked about the experience, they usually comment about not even remembering doing the form or sparring. The reason for this "loss of time" is that their thinking mind dropped away and was replaced with Mu Sim. It should be noted that most martial artists don't consistently enter this state until they have been practicing for 10 years or more and can't enter this state at will until they have been practicing for over 20 years.

> *The mind must always be in the state of 'flowing,' for when it stops anywhere that means the flow is interrupted and it is this interruption that is injurious to the well-being of the mind. In the case of the swordsman, it means death. When the swordsman stands against his opponent, he is not to think of the opponent, nor of himself, nor of his enemy's sword movements. He just stands there with his sword that, forgetful of all technique, is ready only to follow the dictates of the subconscious. The man has effaced himself as the wielder of the sword. When he strikes, it is not the man but the sword in the hand of the man's subconscious that strikes.*
> Takuan Sōhō

Something to think about...

Cho Sim [초 심]
(Beginner Mind)

Before I go into detail about Cho Sim, lets look at the Korean Words themselves. "Cho" comes from the Chinese word "Sho" (初) which means: beginning or primary. 初 is made up of 刀 and 衣. Normally the ideogrammic compound of the character isn't that important but in this case it is. The character "刀" means "knife" and the character "衣" means "outer layers." So in essence, the characters together mean "cutting through the outer layers." "Sim" comes from the Chinese word "Shin" (心) which in this case means: mind. Therefore, Cho Sim means "Beginner Mind" or "The Mind that Cuts through the Outer Layers." By cutting through the outer layers we open ourselves to new knowledge and free ourselves from the barriers (outer layers) that block us from learning new material. 神通並妙用 – How Miraculous This!!!!!!!

A person with Beginner Mind has a mind that is open and willing to learn. This willingness is not dependent on anything. Specifically, it doesn't matter if the material being covered will make the person learning it look good, or the material is fun to learn, or the material, in the opinion of the person learning it, is readily recognized for its importance, or excreta. A person with Beginner Mind always has a total lack of preconceptions of what is being learned. This person learns the material being covered much faster and to a much greater depth than a person that does not have Beginner Mind.

Shunryu Suzuki, a famous Japanese author on meditation, has this to say about Beginner Mind: IN THE BEGINNER'S MIND THERE ARE MANY POSSIBILITIES, IN THE EXPERT'S MIND THERE ARE FEW.

Do you have a Beginner's Mind?

Something to think about...

Kanjuro Shibata XX Sensei
(Rochester, New York)

Bu Dong Sim (부동심)
(Immovable Mind)

"Bu" comes from the Chinese word "Bu" (不) which means: un- (negation prefix). "Dong" comes from the Chinese word "Do" (動) which in this case means: to move or motion. "Sim" comes from the Chinese word "Shin" (心) which in this case means: mind and or heart. Therefore, Bu Dong Sim means "Immovable mind" or "Immovable heart."

Bu Dong Sim is that which allows a martial artist to be impervious to destructive external temptations and to cut through internal delusions, uncontrolled passions and emotions.

Note: Shingon Buddhism, one of the main schools of Japanese Buddhism, has a guardian deity named "Fudo Myoo." "Bu Dong" is Korean for the Japanese "Fudo."

Fudo Myoo is the destroyer of delusion and a principal protector of Buddhism. His immovability refers to that aspect of mind (Buddha Nature), which is forever unmoved - perfectly stable and unchanging. Despite his fearsome appearance, his role is to aid all beings by showing them the true essence of the teachings of the Buddha, leading them into perfect mental discipline. He usually holds a sword and a lariat, is clad in monastic rags, has one fang pointing up and another pointing down, and a braid on the left side of his head. His statues are generally placed near waterfalls and deep in the mountains and in caves.

- Wikipedia contributors. "Acala." *Wikipedia, The Free Encyclopedia.* Wikipedia, The Free Encyclopedia, 4 Feb. 2012. Web. 5 Feb. 2012.

Something to think about...

Author Demonstrating Kyudo at the Memorial Art Gallery
(Rochester, New York)

Jan Sim [잔 심]
(Reflective Mind)

"Jan" comes from the Chinese word "Can" (殘) which means: destroy or demolish. "Sim" comes from the Chinese word "Shin" (心) which in this case means: mind. Therefore, Jan Sim literally means "Demolished Mind." It is that which is left over after an abrupt, powerful (either mental or physical) action: a breaking technique, the end of a form, a loud unexpected noise, etc. Once a martial artist's "mind" has been "destroyed", he is left in a state of heightened, relaxed awareness. When this state is entered for the first time it last only an instant, but with repetition it can last for what seems like an eternity.

In Kyudo, the shot (the release of the arrow) instantly cuts through the mind ("destroys it") and yields Jan Sim. After each shot, the Kyudoka (student) remains absolutely still. During that time, all senses are extremely heightened and the mind is able to reflect back an unbiased assessment of the true quality of the shot. In a lot of ways, Jan Sim and Mu Sim are very similar. Both eliminate conscious thinking, but unlike Mu Sim, Jan Sim communicates to the martial artist through pure impartial thoughts (neither positive nor negative) within an enhanced state of awareness.

Something to think about...

Author practicing Kyudo at the oldest Martial Art Dojo in Japan
(Kyoto, Japan)

Su Pa I (수파이)

The Three Phases of Learning in Taekwondo

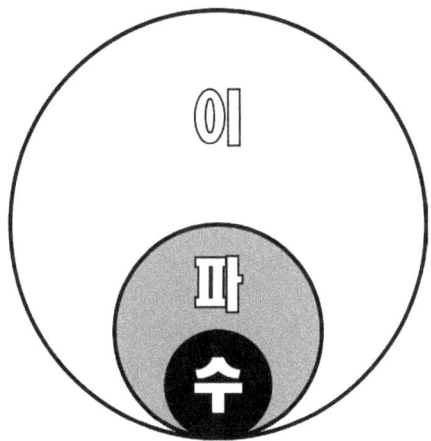

Phase 1: Su (수) - To Defend & Protect

"Su" comes from the Chinese word "Shou" (守) which means: to defend, protect, guard, conserve. 守 is made up of 宀 and 3 additional strokes. The character "宀" means, "roof".

In this phase, new students learn the fundamentals of the art, including the movements, techniques, manners, mental knowledge, etc. It is very important that these students faithfully follow the teachings of their instructor because the student is not ready to explore any modifications.

> *If you believe everything I say, you are a fool. Prove me right or prove me wrong. However, do it my way for now, so you can live long enough to prove me wrong.* - Tom Brown Jr.

Phase 2: Pa (파) – To Break & Destroy

"Pa" comes from the Chinese word "Po" (破) which means: to rupture, break, ruin, destroy. 破 is made up of 石 and 5 additional strokes. The character "石" means, "stone".

In this phase, students are finally ready to learn. In Taekwondo this is typically around the rank of First Degree Black Belt. This is when students start to form their own ideas and start breaking from tradition. From a mental point of view, this is when the students start to make progress cutting through their egos and breaking their attachments to the illusions of self that have formed over their lifetimes. They finally start to realize that the mirror is lying.

Phase 3: I (이) – To Leave

"I" comes from the Chinese word "Li" (離) which means: to leave, depart, go away, separate. 離 is made up of 隹 and 11 additional strokes. The character "隹" means, "bird". It should be noted that 離 is also the character for the third trigram (fire).

In this phase, students have transcended the movements, techniques, manners, mental knowledge, etc. They dwell in the four minds, switching back and forth spontaneously. When practicing a technique, they have no conscious thoughts. Their minds cut through any invasive delusional thoughts. They stand completely aware of their surroundings and are always open to new ideas. They cling to nothing, including their egos, because they have no ego. All their thought-objects disappear and their thinking minds drop away.

For things are things because of mind, as mind is mind because of things. – Xin Xin Ming

Something to think about...

Dokcham

This week I would like to discuss an aspect of meditation that will be added this year to the Winter Retreat. It is called "Dokcham" (독참). "Dok" comes from the Chinese character 獨, which means "alone" or "by oneself". "Cham" comes from the Chinese character 參, which means, "take part in" (It should be noted that the base radical for this Chinese character is 厶, which means "secret"). Together the characters mean, "to enter alone" or "to take part in alone".

Back in the 5th century, Bodhidharma, a Buddhist monk, traveled from India to China to spread Buddhism. Specifically, he brought Chan Buddhism to China. This school focuses on seated meditation and became known as Zen Buddhism when migrated to Japan. In addition to being know as the 1st patriarch of Chan Buddhism, Bodhidharma is widely regarded as the founder of the Shaolin Temple in China. This claim is highly debated, but regardless of whether or not he founded the temple, he did introduce the temple to the practice of martial arts (this is also debated). From the beginning, Chan Buddhism and martial arts have heavily influenced each other and multiple practices have passed from one to the other over the centuries.

During the Tang Dynasty, a monk named Linji Yixuan, founded the Linji School (branch) of Chan Buddhism. The specifics of this branch are not important in regard to this article. What is important is that, due to it forcing a very strict adherence to discipline on its practitioners, it developed an even stronger relationship with the martial arts in China and eventually in Japan and Korea. There are several practices that are unique to Linji Chan that have been adopted by numerous martial arts, one being Dokcham.

It should be noted that even though Dokcham has Buddhist origins, the version used in the various martial traditions, that have adopted it, is similar only in physical form and has no religious significance. Dokcham provides a student the means to privately ask a question or questions of his/her instructor with the knowledge that the question and the answer are private and only shared between the two of them and not the general student/instructor population. In an age of email it might seem like a waste for an instructor to set aside so much time to talk to students privately, when a simple email could easily suffice, but this couldn't be further from the truth. A student normally puts a lot of thought into the question he/she is going to ask before Dokcham, which normally provides for much deeper and meaningful question. Dokcham also gives the instructor a chance to look at the student's body language and behavior while the question is being asked (a lot can be learned about a student with this in conjunction to the actual question being asked).

So, what kind of questions should be asked? That's simple, anything can be asked (well anything related to martial arts). The instructor conducting Dokcham always has the option to simply not answer a question and dismiss the student, if the instructor feels that the question isn't worth answering. For example, a question concerning how to execute a front kick is more appropriately asked in class and would be a waste of the instructor's time to answer it in Dokcham. Typically, questions concerning the mental aspects are asked more so than questions concerning the physical aspects of Martial Arts, but this isn't written in stone. Deeply thought out questions are typically answered no matter what the subject.

Below is an overview of how Dokcham is conducted at my schools and at the retreats I host:

1. Students that want to take part in Dokcham will sit with the retreat participants in morning meditation. Participation in Dokcham is completely optional.
2. At some point during meditation, the instructor that is running Dokcham will ring a hand bell.
3. Once the bell is rung, students that would like to participate in Dokcham should immediately stand and run toward the Dokcham room. The first student to arrive should enter the room, with the remaining students sitting in a line in the predetermined area, in the order in which they arrived. When in line, students should continue meditating until it is their turn to enter the room.
4. Upon entering the Dokcham room, close the door and stand in front of the instructor. Both the instructor and student bow. Then the student should proceed forward to the cushion in front of the instructor and kneel. If the student is a private student of the instructor they should perform a kneeling bow, if not they should simply kneel. Then the student states his or her name and his or her question. The instructor will then proceed to answer his or her question. It is important that the student not interrupt the answer. Most of the time the instructor, when finished, will ask if he/she adequately answered the question. Once the instructor feels Dokcham is over, he/she will ring his/her hand bell. At that point the student is to rise, straighten the cushion, walk backwards to the place they initially bowed, bow and then leave the room, leaving the door open. Once the student exits the room, the student should quietly return to his/her initial meditation spot with the rest of the retreat participants.
5. The student in the front of the line, waiting to enter the Dokcham room, should ring the gong 2 times upon hearing the instructor's hand bell, being rung to dismissing the student that is currently in the Dokcham room. How the gong is rung will provide the instructor with a wealth of information on the quality of the entering student's mind. It is therefore important to not simple ring the bell but to mindfully ring the bell.

6. This process continues until the last student in line rings the bell (3 times – signals the last student is entering). If time runs out before everyone in the Dokcham line has had a chance to ask their question, the meditation monitor will send back all the students remaining in line to the general meditation area, except the student at the front of the line.

Always put a lot of thought into the question you are going to ask during Dokcham and don't waste everyone's time by asking "how to get more flexible?"

Something to think about...

Daruma Doll

Dukcham (My First Experience)

Several days ago I came across a journal that had a very large section devoted to my first experiences with meditation. Reading through it I found an account of my first Dukcham experience. It should be noted that this was a Japanese based Meditation Retreat and I was a teenager.

"Ding…..Ding…..Ding….. Ruuuuuuuuuuuuuunnnnnnnnnnnnnn. I can't believe there is only one person in front of me! How did that happen? Up the stairs. Oh no, I tripped. Get up! Run! She (the person in front of me) goes in to see Sensei first, that means I'm first in line. I hope my breathing slows down before the bell rings."

"Ding….Ding….Ding…. Ok, now it's my turn. Ding. Ding. I hope I didn't hit the bell to hard. Well here goes nothing. Close the door. Walk over in front of Sensei, on the edge of the carpet, and bow. Walk up and kneel. "My name is Sean Pearson. My practice is following my breath?""

"Ding….Ding….Ding….Ding…. Bow and leave. That wasn't so bad." Well that is exactly how it was written in the journal. What I didn't mention is that I had arrived late to the meditation hall that day. Because I was late, I had to sit a long way away from the door that people participating in Dokcham had to exit (run) through when the bell was rung. There were a half-dozen people between that door and me. I remember the bell ringing and the next thing I remember was being half way up the stairs, climbing over another student trying to get to the top first. I have no idea of how I got to be second in line. I have no memory of traveling from my meditation cushion. It was a truly amazing experience.

Something to think about…

Kanjuro Shibata XX Sensei
(Kyoto, Japan)

Jumu – To Work & Serve

For this article I thought I would talk about the "work" everyone does at the retreats I host. In an effort to offer more traditional retreats, several years ago I started to assign people "chores" to be done at the retreats.

These "chores" are called Jumu (주무) in Korean. Ju (주) is the hanja for the Chinese word 作 (Zuò), which means "to work". Mu (무) is the hanja for the Chinese word 務 (Wu), which means "service".

This assigning of work accomplishes two goals. The first being that of strengthening the groups bonding. When the participants all "pitch in" to help, the retreat becomes more of an event they are helping to run, as opposed to an event that they are attending. The second, and for me most important reason, is to "just work". As I mentioned in other articles, anything can be a meditative practice and in the case of the "chores" they become a meditative practice by "just working".

If the work is carried out wakefully, in a manner based entirely on the activity of collected attention and total carefulness, then it is a continuation and another form of meditative practice, in which the practitioner learns to maintain the meditative state of mind even in the midst of everyday routine.
- The Shambhala Dictionary

When a student enters the Dojang (training floor), they all enter wearing uniforms. There is no distinction between them. Everyone is the same, other than the student's Taekwondo rank. A doctor stands next to a janitor who stands next to a teacher who stands next to the president of a Fortune 500 company. They all look the same and are treated the same. The outside world is left behind when they step onto the training floor. This is also true for Jumu. Every "chore" has the same value. One isn't any better than any other and therefore all should be approached with the same enthusiasm. Cleaning the hall floor should be just as important as cooking the food, which should be just as important as serving tea. No one has a better Jumu. As soon as someone feels their "chore" is easier or better than another student's, they have failed.

Once the student receives their "chore" at a retreat, they should be grateful for the chance to contribute and not think, "Yes, I got ....." or "No, I don't want that...".

Just work.......

Something to think about...

What is a Kihap?

기합

This article took some thought. Not because I didn't know what to write about but because my views on the subject, especially within the Taekwondo community, might not be viewed in a favorable light. I want to talk about the Kihap 기합 (Kiai in Japanese). For those of you that don't know, it is the "yell" you hear martial artists making during sparring, forms, breaking, etc. The word Kihap comes from two Chinese characters: 氣合. Qi (氣) means "breath" or "spirit" and is commonly translated as "energy" in English. Hé (合) means "to combine", "to unite" or "to join". The two radicals that combine to form "合" are "亼", meaning to assemble or to gather together, and "口", meaning mouth (interesting). So Kihap literally means, "to unite energy".

(It should be noted that Japanese Martial Artists use 気, a simplified version of 氣)

A Kihap is a vocal exhalation emanating from the danjeon 단전, the energy center of the body (a future article). If you ask several masters, "Why do we Kihap?", you will get several answers. None of them are wrong but if you only listen to one or two of them, the benefits of Kihaping will be greatly decreased. So what are these reasons?

- intimidating an opponent
- focusing (both mind and body)
- forcing an exhalation
- psych oneself up
- and more……

If a martial artist only views a Kihap as a way of intimidating an opponent or psyching himself up, any loud noise will do. It is truly amazing the variety of very loud and very scary sounds you hear at martial art tournaments (some are more funny than scary – maybe they want their opponents to laugh). The problem is that only about a quarter of these Kihaps can be correctly used to force a free-flowing exhalation or to improve focus. Why? Because, only Kihaps ending in a vowel (there are a very few exceptions to this) do not restrict the flow of the breath on the exhalation. Try it. Try making some of the various Kihaps you have heard. If they end in a consonant, you will feel a restriction in your exhalation. A correct Kihap must end in a vowel. Whenever there is a restricted airflow, there is a potential to damage the lungs (Pulmonary Barotrauma). Think about it this way, take a large balloon and place a very small hole in it (so that the air is exiting the balloon but slowly). Now sit on the balloon. What happens? It pops even though air is coming out of the balloon. Now I realize that this is a far cry from someone slightly restricting his/her airflow, by Kihaping incorrectly, and that your lungs are not going to pop, but it isn't very difficult to injure them. Think about all the pressure a martial artist's muscles place on the lungs when executing a technique, or when they hit a stack of bricks or when an opponent kicks them, any restriction in the airflow can cause damage to the lungs.

My schools teach three basic Kihaps. Each one is used with a specific class of techniques and all of them end in vowels.

- The first Kihap is "Ā". It sounds like the word "eight" without the "t" on the end.
- The second Kihap is "Ō". It sounds like the word "oh".
- The third Kihap is "Ē". It sounds like "eeeeeeee".

The easiest way to describe the techniques these Kihaps are used for is by looking at three different strikes with a short stick. If you put the end of the stick on a target and push, the second Kihap is used. If you hit the target with a fast out and back motion with the stick, the third Kihap is used. If you hit the target but don't retract the stick after impact or hit through the target before retracting the stick, the first Kihap is used.

Side Note: If you reverse the two Chinese characters for Kihap, 氣合, you get Hapki 合氣, or Aiki in Japanese, as in Hapkido, or Aikido in Japanese.

Something to think about...

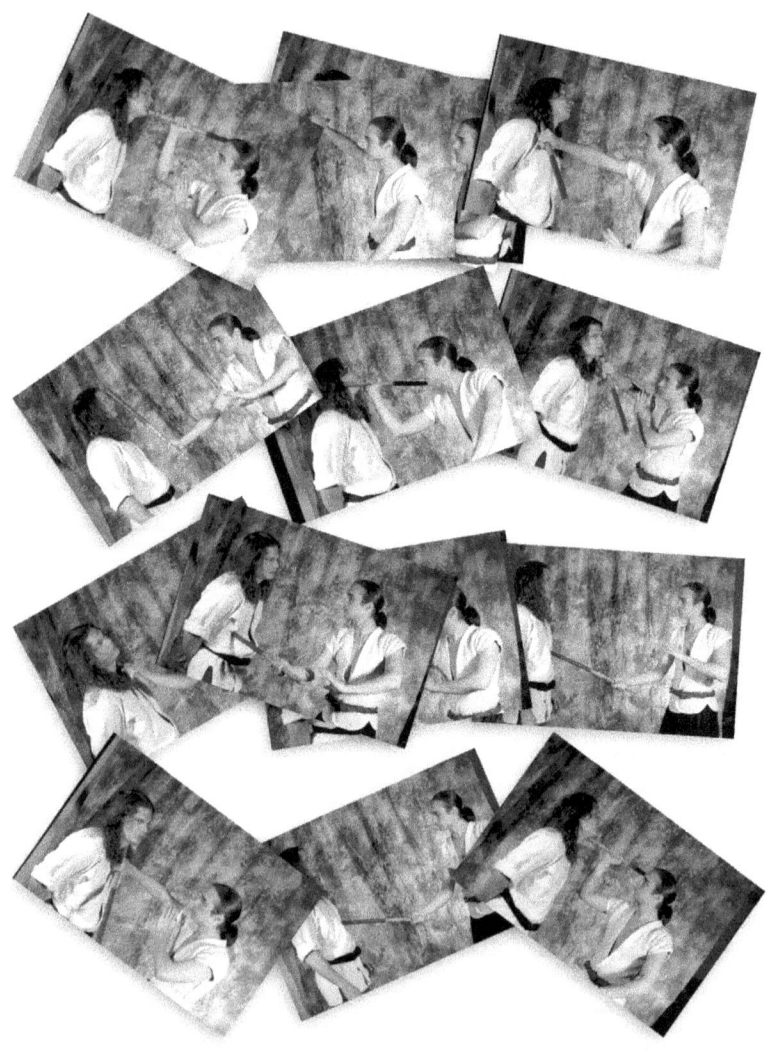

Author Demonstrating 10 Basic Stick Butt Strikes with Sensei Larry White
(Early 1990's)

Sim Sin Dan Yeon – Jeong Sin Su Yang

I am frequently asked about the Chinese characters that are on my students' black belts (3rd Dan and up). I thought that for this article I would answer these questions.

I do not allow any of my black belts to wear rank tips on their belts (why is another article). However, in the 90's I decided that it would be nice to have something on our belts in place of tips. It didn't take me long to decide what to put on them. Back when I worked with Grandmaster Ahn, I would constantly run into two sets of Chinese Characters, mostly when I would look at his old photos. When I would ask him about the meanings of these characters, he would usually give me a very brief and vague translation. So, eventually I decided that if I wanted to find out what these characters meant, I would have to do a little work on my own. This is how Grandmaster Ahn has taught me from the first day I started working for him. He intentionally would give me vague answers, so I would have to figure things out for myself. Then once I did, he would answer my question and talk to me about what I came up with and why it was different (if it was).

Below is a couple of old pictures and one brochure with these two sets of characters. It should be mentioned that these characters were also on the entrances of his old schools.

First Set:

心 – This is the Chinese character Xin and is pronounced Sim (심) in Korean. It means (in this context): heart and/or mind.

身- This is the Chinese character Shen and is pronounced Sin (신) in Korean. It means (in this context): body.

鍛- This is the Chinese character Duan and is pronounced Dan (단) in Korean. It means (in this context): to forge or temper.

練- This is the Chinese character Lian and is pronounced Yeon (연) in Korean. It means (in this context): to practice.

Together these characters mean: To forge the body and mind through practice.

Second Set:

精 – This is the Chinese character Jing and is pronounced Jeong (정) in Korean. It means (in this context): energy.

神 - This is the Chinese character Shen and is pronounced Sin (신) in Korean. It means (in this context): spirit.

修 – This is the Chinese character Xiu and is pronounced Su (수) in Korean. It means (in this context): to cultivate.

養 – This is the Chinese character Yang and is pronounced Yang (양) in Korean. It means (in this context): to grow.

Together these characters mean: To cultivate and grow energy and spirit.

So as a whole, taken in the context of Taekwondo, they mean:

> *"Through the practice of Taekwondo an individual will forge their bodies and minds, and will grow and cultivate their energy and spirit."*

This is just one possible translation. I encourage all of you to translate these characters yourself and see what you come up with. After all, you learn more by discovering the answer to a question yourself than having it handed to you.

Something to think about...

Image/Photo Citations

Photo 1:   Gup Belts – Sara Kitchen – 04/09/2011

Knife Seminar held at Ahn Taekwondo Institute (Cincinnati, Ohio)
Photos taken by Sara Kitchen

A Fundamental Flaw in the Trigrams

Back in the early 90's, I was Dan Director for the US Taekwondo Union and in addition to taking care of all the Kukkiwon Dan and Poom certifications for the US, I was also tasked with promoting the martial art side of Taekwondo. To that end, I wrote an article for the Taekwondo Times on the Trigrams and the Taegeuk Forms. I had spoken on the subject several times before that and Grandmaster Ahn, the President of the USTU at the time, encouraged me to write on the subject for the Times so that more people would have access to the information. I had no idea how much of a splash that article was going to make. Within days of it being published, my phone started ringing. Everyone from color belts to grandmasters were calling me and asking questions about the Trigrams. I would even have people at tournaments walk up to me and after the comment, "you're the one that wrote the article on the Trigrams," would start asking all sorts of questions.

The interest the general body of Taekwondo practitioners showed toward them only made me want to explore them even more. So began my quest to know everything there was to know about the Trigrams. I thought it was going to be a life long journey, but it was only a short walk. After a couple of year's of reading everything I could on the Trigrams and looking at them from every point of view I could think of, I was stumped. As far as I could tell there was nothing else to learn. I thought, "I'm must be missing something," but I didn't know what it was. So, what is a good Taekwondo instructor to do? The only thing I could, I assigned several long projects to a few of my black belts to hopefully get them to discover what I was missing. Guess what, they discovered nothing. One of my black belts, after an entire summer of working on one problem said, "they're just three lines, nothing else." I had her make an elaborate wheel for generating Trigram combinations (the statistician in me was coming out) and she was supposed to record the results. After she had pages of Trigram combinations, she was unable to learn anything.

Years went by with no breakthroughs. Then just the other day I was sitting in Starbucks and thinking about the Trigrams. I wonder how many people have "Grande, extra hot lattes" in Starbucks and think about trigrams? Anyway, I was and then Andrew Wood popped into my head. Who is Andrew Wood you ask? Before MAIA or NAMPA (both martial art industry associations), Mr. Wood was the only person out there that had a program to help martial art school owners make their schools more successful. One of his suggestions, that drastically changed how I taught Taekwondo, was to write a curriculum for a student from white belt all the way to black belt. This wasn't just an overview, but a list of everything you would teach, for every class, from white belt to black belt. He suggested that anyone that was going to undertake this assignment should get a hotel room for the weekend and basically lock himself or herself inside until it was done. So that is exactly what I did. Back then; the Kukkiwon had a 300-class (hour) requirement for promotion to black belt, from white belt. When I was finished I had 300 index cards for every class a student would take from white to black belt. Each card had not only every technique I would teach the student, but also how much time I would spend on each technique. I am so happy I did that. So what changed after I finished my 300 cards? More than you can possibly imagine (I think I'll have that be another article).

Anyway, as I was sitting in Starbucks, thinking about Andrew Wood, I thought, "what if I started from the beginning and imagine that the Trigrams didn't exist yet. How would I have developed them?" So that is what I did. Started with Um (Yin) and Yang and reinvented the Trigrams. What I came up with wasn't the same as the original Trigrams and it gave me a huge insight into the Trigrams that I had never seen before.

The Trigrams each have three lines, made up of two different lines: a solid line (yang) and a dashed line (um). As any good statistician would know, the "Fundamental Counting Rule" tells us that if event x can occur X ways and event y can occur Y ways, then both events together can occur X * Y ways. Therefore, because each of the three lines has two possibilities, there are 8 Trigrams (2 * 2 * 2 = 8). The idea behind these Trigrams is that they are supposed to reflect the Way of Nature. Unfortunately, they don't and here is why and therefore the fundamental flaw the Trigrams have.

As I am writing this article, I'm sitting in my car waiting for my wife to finish volunteering at a fundraiser. The wind is blowing and the trees are moving. They are exhibiting one of nature's most basic truths: there are no right angles in nature. I don't mean that literally. What I mean is that when the trees swing back and forth, they don't instantly change directions form one direction to the other. Instead they move toward the one extreme and slow down as they reach it. Then without even stopping they start moving the other direction. Like they are tracing a circle. Ok, maybe more of an eclipse, but never an instant change from one direction to the other. Watch nature; watch your breathing, watch people move, everything moves in a flowing motion. Is it possible to produce a motion that doesn't move in this circular fashion? Yes, but is it natural? No. Most people don't breathe correctly and therefore they breathe in and then instantly breathe out. This is an unnatural and inefficient way of breathing. As my Black Belts will tell you, I spend a lot of time teaching them how to breath correctly (naturally), with no sudden changes. How do you do that? Watch a baby breathe and then you will know.

So what does this have to do with the Trigrams? As I said before, the lines of the Trigrams only have two options, pure Um or pure Yang and when they change from one to the other they change instantly. This isn't natural and is the flaw in the Trigrams. There should be a third option: the infinitesimally small transition period between um transforming into yang or yang transforming into um. The transition between the in breath and the out breath. The transition between to tree swinging one direction, in the wind, to the other direction. The rounded point in everything that undergoes change. This third option is harmony or balance.

With this transition option of balance added to pure yang and pure um, there would be 27 Trigrams instead of 8 (3 * 3 * 3 = 27). These new Trigrams are a much better representation of nature's true nature (in my opinion). All the original Trigrams are still contained in the new 27.

It is important to note that when I went through the creation process, once again using the tools I teach in statistics, the original 8 Trigrams are in exactly the same order as they were originally.

The new set of Trigrams, like the old set, has different arrangements. However, unlike the old set that only has two (earlier heaven and later heaven) arrangements, the new set has several (for future articles). Below is the evolution arrangement of the new Trigrams. In this new set, Um is represented by a dark circle and Yang is represented by a light circle. Balance/Harmony is represented by an unfilled circle (in this case, white). I used circles instead of lines to better conform to the circular nature of things. They are read in a counter clockwise circle.

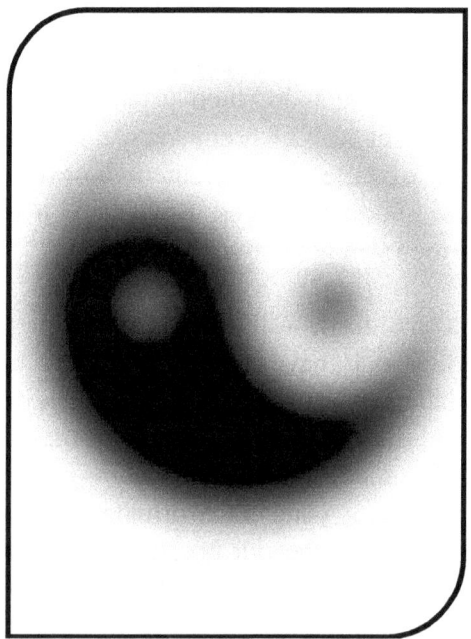

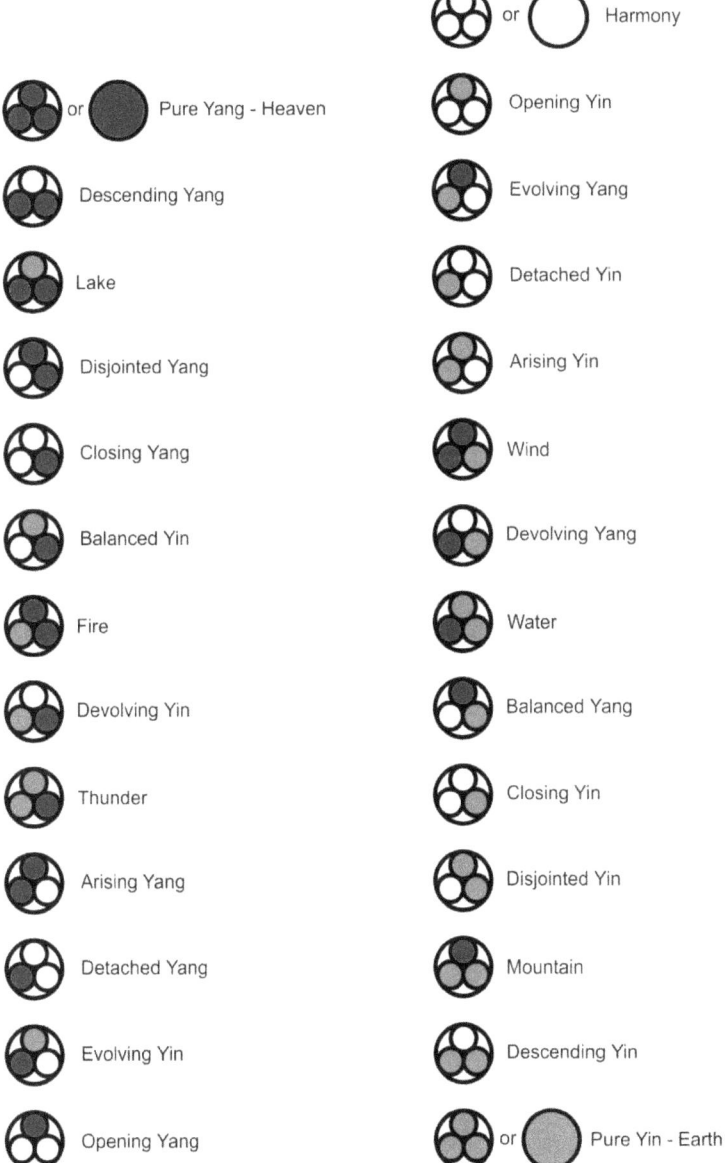

Something to think about...

Author Executing a Staff Form
(Rochester, New York)

Body

Five Direction Open Palm Set

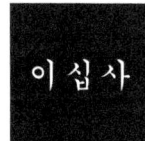

오픈 야자 세트

Most Asian cultures base their understanding of the body and its potential on the concept of ki (chi), a vital-life force or energy, which permeates the world and every living thing. Although ki is a metaphysical concept it can be physically quantified, measured, manipulated, and felt in one's body through various ki practices, one of which is outlined below.

The purpose of these practices is to restore and maintain one's ki in a state of balance. When it is in a proper state of balance, ki moves freely throughout the space or the body that it inhabits and supports the health of that body rather than fighting against it. Balancing this energy is a crucial part of living a healthy and calm life and ki practices such as Five Direction Open Palm Set, the Eight Trigram Exercises, acupuncture or acupressure have been linked to improved health and well-being, increased focus and energy, and reduced levels of stress-related discomfort. From a martial arts perspective, the practice of energy work has tremendous benefits; from strengthening the body to resist blows and strikes to increasing awareness of an opponent's presence.

Directions for the Five Direction Open Palm Set

Ready Position: Stand with your feet shoulder width apart, hands/arms hanging in a natural position and take several abdominal breaths.

Direction One (Down): Lift hands up to solar-plexus height in front of body. Turn hands over and move hands to side of body, palms facing down. Slowly move hands down to side of body, palms still facing down, as if pushing something. This motion should be executed, in conjunction with one Yang Breath.

Direction Two (Sides): Lift hands up to solar-plexus height in front of body. Turn hands over and move hands to side of body, palms out to respective sides of the body. Slowly move hands out, palms still facing out and fingers pointing up, as if pushing something. This motion should be executed, in conjunction with one Yang Breath.

Direction Three (Up): Lift hands up to solar-plexus height in front of body. Turn hands over and move hands to side of body, palms facing up. Slowly move hands up, palms still facing upward and fingers pointing toward each other, as if pushing something. This motion should be executed, in conjunction with one Yang Breath.

Direction Four (Back): Lift hands up to solar-plexus height in front of body. Turn hands over and move hands to side of body, palms facing down. Slowly move hands down to side of body, palms still facing back. Continue motion by slightly moving hands back as if pushing something. This motion should be executed, in conjunction with one Yang Breath.

Direction Five (Front): Lift hands up to solar-plexus height in front of body. Turn hands over and move hands to side of body, palms facing front. Slowly move hands forward, palms still facing front and fingers pointing up, as if pushing something. This motion should be executed, in conjunction with one Yang Breath.

Repeat: Repeat all five directions, five more times (the five directions should be preformed a total of six times).

Ready Position: Stand with your feet shoulder width apart, hands/arms hanging in a natural position and take several abdominal breaths.

Note: The speed at which the directions are preformed is based on the speed of the Yang Breath. The Yang Breathing should be done as slowly as possible without straining the body. When "pushing", the mind should imagine that a heavy object is being pushed and that the muscles are flexed. This should not be the case however. The muscles should always remain in as relaxed of a state as possible.

For those of you that are not familiar with the "Yang Breathing Technique", below is a short overview of the technique:

Yang Breathing (양 호흡)

Application: Used to move Ki out into limbs.

1. As quickly as possible, inhale a full inhalation through the nose (without tensing body).
2. Slowly exhale through the mouth. The exhalation should be a long as possible.
3. Repeat.

Something to think about...

Old B/W Pictures of Grandmaster Kyongwon Ahn

Footwork Patterns

Over the course of this last year I have been spending a lot of time working on footwork patterns with my black belts. This article is a detailed look at what these black belts have already worked on and I am hoping you will also spend some time learning.

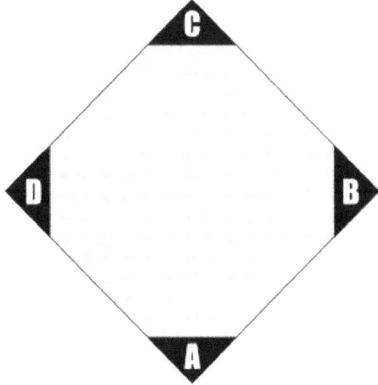

Footwork Patterns are the very foundation of every real world self-defense and classroom two-person confrontation. Without good footwork, everything becomes less effective and efficient: kick, strikes, blocks, joint locks and throws. It is essential that every Taekwondo student have a working knowledge and a good level of proficiency in all six basic footwork patterns.

Footwork Pattern #1	Footwork Pattern #2
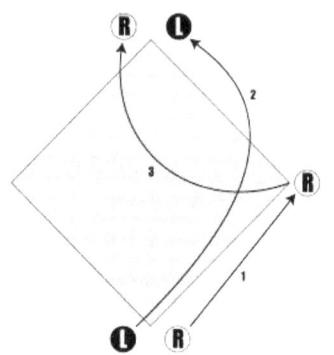	
1) Step with right foot from corner "A" to corner "B".	1) Step with right foot from corner "A" to corner "B".
2) Step with left foot from corner "A" to corner "C", bringing it close to the right foot when stepping.	2) Step with left foot from corner "A" to corner "C", bringing it close to the right foot when stepping.
3) Step with right foot from corner "B" to corner "C".	3) Circular step with the right foot from corner "B" to corner "C".

Footwork Pattern #3	Footwork Pattern #4
1) Step with left foot from corner "A" to corner "B". 2) Step with right foot from corner "A" to corner "C. 3) Step with left foot from corner "B" to corner "C".	1) Step with left foot from corner "A" to corner "B". 2) Circular step with right foot from corner "A" to corner "C. 3) Step with left foot from corner "B" to corner "C".

Footwork Pattern #5	Footwork Pattern #6
1) Step with right foot from corner "A" to corner "B". 2) In a circular motion, bring left foot up to right foot and then back to the center of corner "A". 3) Step with left foot from the center of corner "A" to corner "C". 4) Step with right foot from corner "B" to corner "C".	1) Circular step with left foot from corner "A" to corner "B". 2) Step with right foot from corner "A" to corner "C". 3) Step with left foot from corner "B" to corner "C".

Something to think about...

Beginning Qi (Chi) Training

"It takes 2 years of practice to actually feel the energy and another 2 years to believe that what you are feeling is really energy and not your imagination." – Grandmaster Mantak Chia

I had just driven 6 hours down to New York City, walked around one block of Manhattan for at least 30 minutes before I finally found the building that I was supposed to be taking a Chi Kung (energy work) class in. That wasn't the end of the long trip however, because I couldn't find the entrance to the martial art school that was hosting the seminar. I looked and looked with no luck. Finally I started watching the people around the building. Everyone looked like business people or tourists. Finally, I saw someone who looked out-of-place (maybe a Chi Kung student in the middle of the previously mentioned business people and tourists). So I followed her. She went down something I guess you could call an alley (actually it looked like a hallway without a door). So down the alley I went, I turned left at a dumpster (not really), went through an unmarked door and up several flights of stairs. Just before I almost decided to turn around I was standing in a martial art school and was being asked, "Are you here for the Chi Kung seminar?" I guess location is everything.

Believe it or not, I was early and had 30 or so minutes to kill. I walked around, looked at all the posters on the walls and realized I was the only one there that didn't know everyone else that was attending the seminar. The seminar started on time with the instructor introducing himself and saying, "It takes 2 years of practice to actually feel the energy and another 2 years to believe that what you are feeling is really energy and not your imagination." I thought, "Great, I'll be almost 30 years old before I can actually do this stuff. That's really old." Almost 20 years later, I now know that 30 isn't really that old and that I don't believe the quote is true. It does however offer a new student an indication as to how much work is ahead of them and that is why I use it when I teach.

This article is going to cover the first exercise I teach to all of my black belts that undertake Chi Kung training. Students using this exercise have reported great success after only a very short period of time. It will also benefit students that have no desire to do energy work by increasing awareness of their bodies (be warned that people who practice this technique have reported being kept awake at night by the feeling of blood pumping through my bodies). Simply put, this practice consists of feeling the pulse in the dominate hand's little finger by simply looking at it and feeling the blood "pulsing" in it. "Why would I want to be able to do that and how is that going to help with anything?" is what most of you are thinking. Because, once you can feel the pulse in your little finger, with a little practice you will be able to feel it in any part of the body. This then leads to the ability to feel it simultaneously in multiple parts of the body. Once a student has developed the sensitivity to feel blood circulating through the body, the process of starting to feel and eventually direct the Ki (Chi/energy) is much faster and easier.

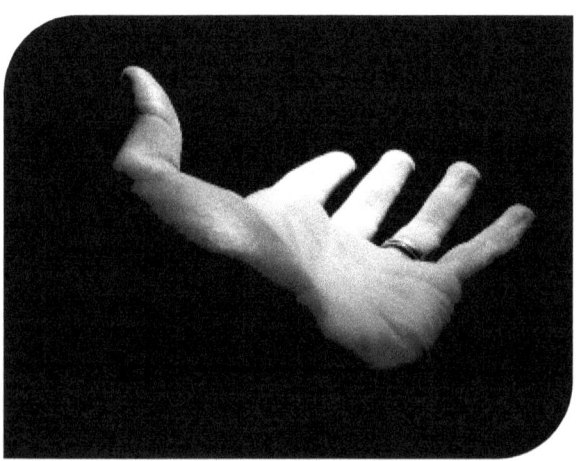

The Exercise:

1. Start by taking your pulse on your wrist the traditional way with two fingers. At the same time focus your mind on the little finger on the same hand.
2. At first "imagine" you can feel the pulse in your little finger beating with the pulse on your wrist.
3. Slowly let up pressure with your fingers on the wrist so that you can barely feel your pulse. Continue to feel (imagine) the pulse in your little finger. If you start losing the imagined feeling in your little finger, simply press harder with the two fingers on your wrist, then reestablish the feeling again.
4. After you are able to feel the imagined pulse for an extended period of time, completely remove the two fingers from you wrist. Continue to feel the pulse for at least 30 seconds. Replace fingers on wrist and see if the imagined and real pulse match.
5. Once you can consistently match the pulses, increase the time your fingers are off your wrist to 60 seconds.
6. Continue increasing the length of time until you are able to consistently feel your pulse in your little finger without the need of using your wrist pulse.

Eventually, you will be able to simply focus on your little finger and feel your pulse. Once you are able to do that, pick other parts of your body and with a little practice you will be able to feel it there also. The next step is to focus on the area between two places that you can readily feel the pulse. Feel the blood flowing from the one point to the other. Over time you will be able to feel blood flowing through your entire body. If you ever doubt your ability, simple tap out your pulse with your foot and then take your pulse the traditional way. If they match, maybe the next time you won't doubt your abilities.

Something to think about...

Old B/W Pictures of Grandmaster Kyongwon Ahn

Breathing

General Overview

The below eight breathing methods represent the core breathing techniques within my schools and are only a portion of the methods contained within their curriculum. Unless otherwise indicated, the tip of the tongue should touch the roof of the mouth right behind the teeth and the entire body should be relaxed as possible during the breathing method being implemented.

Abdominal Breathing (aka. Diaphragmatic Breathing)

Application: The primary/default breathing method used by most Taekwondo practitioners.

1. Inhale through the nose into the lungs in such a way as to expand the abdomen and not the chest.
2. Exhale through the mouth (or the nose when not engaged in physical exertion).
3. Repeat.

Note: The chest should not move at all during this style of breathing. This breathing method should not be confused with Replete Breathing where the chest does move. Advanced practitioners of this breathing method will not only expand the front of the abdomen when inhaling but they will also expand the sides and back as well.

Replete Breathing

Application: Used to increase focus and reduce stress.

1. Inhale through the nose into the lungs in such a way as to completely expand the abdomen and not the chest.
2. Continue to inhale through the nose in such a way as to completely expand the chest.
3. Exhale through the mouth in such a way as to completely contract the abdomen and not the chest.
4. Continue to exhale through the mouth is such a way as to completely contract the chest.
5. Repeat.

Yang Breathing

Application: Used to move ki (chi) out into limbs.

1. As quickly as possible, inhale a full inhalation through the nose (without tensing body).
2. Slowly exhale through the mouth. The exhalation should be a long as possible.
3. Repeat.

Yin Breathing

Application: Used to move ki (chi) into trunk of body.

1. Slowly inhale a full inhalation through the nose. The inhalation should be a long as possible.
2. As quickly as possible exhale through the mouth.
3. Repeat.

Square Breathing

Application: Used to relax body and mind.

1. Slowly inhale a full inhalation through the nose while counting from one to four.
2. Hold breath for a count of 4.
3. Slowly exhale a full exhalation through the mouth while counting from one to four.
4. Hold breath for a count of 4.
5. Repeat.

Triangle Breathing (aka. 4 - 7 - 8 Breathing)

Application: Used to relax body and mind.

1. Slowly inhale a full inhalation through the nose while counting from one to four.
2. Hold breath for a count of 7.
3. Slowly exhale a full exhalation through the mouth while counting from one to eight.
4. Repeat.

Bellows Breathing

Application: Used to stimulate the body and mind.

1. Inhale and exhale as quickly as possible through the nose. Each inhalation and exhalation should be as short as possible and equal in length. Repeat for 10 seconds.
2. Breath deeply for 50 seconds.
3. Repeat.

Reverse Breathing

Application: Used as part of some Chi Kung Exercises.

1. Slowly inhale through the mouth while contracting in the abdomen (without tensing the muscles).
2. Slowly exhale through the nose while expanding the abdomen (without tensing the muscles).
3. Repeat.

Something to think about...

The Boards

When people visit one of my schools they inevitably inquire about the various strange looking boards that are lying around. This article is all about those boards, which are used for training.

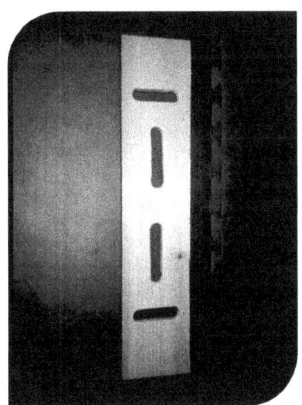

Board 1

This board is a 1" x 5" x 30" with 4 slots cut into it. As you can see in the above picture the slots are symmetrical. There is one vertical and one horizontal slot on each end of the board. To use this board a student has to stand at a distance that will allow the hand to pass half way through the slot when the arm is fully extended. The student stands perpendicular to the board, which is held by another student at shoulder height. Eight pierces are then executed. Alternating right and left hands. Below is the piercing sequence:

Pierce #1: Right hand into right vertical slot (thumb on top)
Pierce #2: Left hand into left vertical slot (thumb on top)
Pierce #3: Right hand into right horizontal slot (palm down)
Pierce #4: Left hand into left horizontal slot (palm down)
Pierce #5: Right hand into right vertical slot (thumb on bottom)
Pierce #6: Left hand into left vertical slot (thumb on bottom)

Pierce #7: Right hand into right horizontal slot (palm up)
Pierce #8: Left hand into left horizontal slot (palm up)

Note: Students are required to bend their fingers after they pass through the slot (see picture):

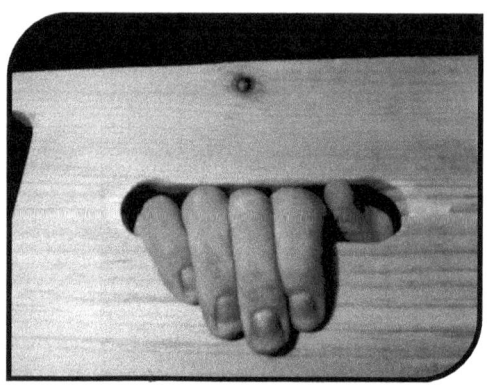

So now the why: This exercise helps develop three abilities. The first and most obvious is accuracy. If the student's pierces are off by even a fraction of an inch, his/her fingers will hit the wood instead of passing thought the slot. After only practicing with this board for a short period of time, students will see a drastic decline in the number of times they hit their fingers. Keep in mind that the slots are only 1" wide. As stated above, a student practicing with this board must bend his/her fingers after they pass through the slot. This bending helps develop the second ability, the capability to judge distance. If the student bends his/her fingers before they pass through the slot, the knuckles will hit the board and if the student doesn't straighten his/her fingers before the hand is withdrawn, the hand will get stuck. The final ability this exercise helps develop is self-confidence. When a student first starts working with the board they execute the pierces very slowly, unless properly motivated, because they don't have the confidence that they can truly put their hand exactly where they want it to go. With practice, a student will be able to execute pierces very quickly with accuracy, flawless judgment of distance and with correct timing and therefore improved self-confidence.

Board 2

This board is used in exactly the same manner as the first board except for the fact that only one finger is passed through the board. This board (10" x 10" x 1") has nine holes:

At first, students alternate piercing the center hole with their right and left index fingers. Like with the above board, the index finger is bent after it passes through the hole:

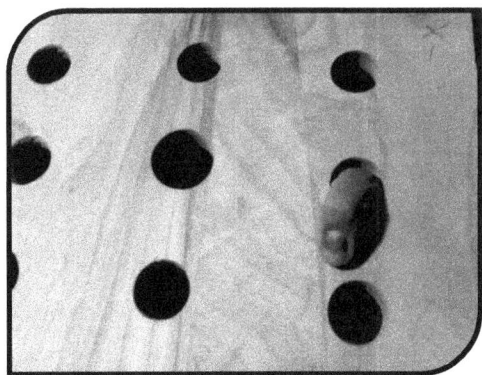

Once a student can consistently perform the pierces through the center hole (1.25"), without hitting the wood with the index finger, he/she moves on to the smaller holes (1"). The student executes two pierces (one right and one left) on each of the 8 smaller holes and then repeats the desired number of times. The benefits of this exercise are the same as the ones mentioned above.

When a student can consistently pass through all the holes without hitting the wood, a piece of copy paper is placed between two boards with matching holes (the pink paper in picture):

With the paper in place, the student must commit to executing the pierce with force in order to break through the paper. The thickness of the paper is increased with the student's proficiency.

So that's an overview of the boards used in the first weekend. I hope the information will prove useful and that some of you will make your own set of boards.

Something to think about...

Another Board with both Finger & Hand Holes

Culture

Natto

Over the years, I have repeatedly had a very specific conversation with various students and instructors. This conversation was about my belief that in order for a person to be a well-rounded martial artist they had to immerse themselves into the culture of the country that the martial art they practice was from. I am in no way saying that they need to become Korean, Japanese, Chinese, etc. or that they have to act like they are Korean, Japanese, Chinese, etc. What I am saying is that a martial artist should basically have a working understanding of the culture of their art's country of origin through a "hands on" approach. It was, after all, that culture that defined the art and made it what it is today. This belief of mine comes from the first Taekwondo School I attended. They required that I be able to use chopsticks before I could take my black belt exam. At that time in my life, I thought it was a ridiculous skill to require and had nothing to do with Taekwondo. I was told I had to learn to use them because as a black belt I would be eating with Korean Masters from time to time and that I would offend them if I used a fork to eat my food. Seriously? What a ridiculous reason, but a requirement was a requirement and I learned how to use them. Regardless of the reason, I still use them today and prefer them to a fork.

Around the same time, I visited the home of Grandmaster Kyongwon Ahn with Master Van Hee (a Master Instructor at one of my schools but back then he was simply Jim). Mrs. Ahn was very kind to us and brought out a bowl of Kimchi (she makes the best Kimchi I have ever had and I have had a lot of Kimchi). It should be noted that I had already had Kimchi but Master Van Hee hadn't. Mrs. Ahn, upon setting the bowl down, said, "It's hot." Master VanHee assuming she meant "temperature hot" and not "spicy hot", immediately shoveled a very large fork-full (yes she had forks) into his mouth. The look on his face was priceless. It took him tremendous willpower not to run to the bathroom and spit it out. He had thought it was cooked cabbage with barbecue sauce. Today he loves Kimchi, but back then....

I could go on and on with stories of how I learned about different cultural customs, manners, foods, etc. but I want to write a series of articles on these topics and not just one. Looking back over the years at how I learned these various things, I was yelled at after offending people, laughed at after making a fool out of myself, praised because I knew something that was deemed something I shouldn't have known, and I enjoyed every minute of it. These are the things that the people who invented the arts we practice, lived with on a daily basis and make no mistake about it, they influenced the creation of those arts. Now, is it absolutely essential to know how to use chopsticks in order to be a good black belt? No! However, it is the popcorn, hotdogs and soda that make attending a baseball game enjoyable. Can you imagine going to a game and not having the people selling all those incredibly delicious items? I can't. Those simple foods are what make going to a game a complete experience, even though they really have nothing directly to do with baseball.

For my first article in this series I picked a Japanese food that is either a "love it" or "hate it" food for most people: Natto.

I was first exposed to Natto on one of my weeklong visits to Kanjuro Shibata XX Sensei's House in Boulder, CO. In addition to watching me practicing Kyudo every day, Sensei would cook at least one meal a day for me. I would always offer to cook but he would make a face, shake his head and say "no." Not that I am complaining because he is an amazing cook. There will be a few more articles about other foods he exposed me to, in future books. Anyway, back to the Natto. It was lunchtime and Sensei and I were sitting at a table outside, under a big tree. David, Sensei's live-in assistant at the time, brought out three bowls of rice and three odd-looking Styrofoam square boxes.

I should have known something was up when David sat down with a huge grin on his face. Sensei was also looking very mischievous (well as mischievous as a living Samurai can be anyway). I opened the Styrofoam and found a layer of brownish soybeans covered with plastic wrap, a pouch of soy sauce and a pouch of mustard. So acting like I knew exactly what I was doing, I removed the two pouches and took off the plastic wrap. If they thought I was "in the know" up to that point, they knew I wasn't as soon as the smell hit my nose (it smells like really really smelly cheese). They then both started laughing (well Sensei did this really cool Samurai sort of chuckle). I was then instructed on the finer art of how to eat Natto.

Historically, storing steamed soybeans in rice straw, which naturally contains B. subtilis natto, made Natto. The soybeans were packed in this straw and left to ferment. The fermentation was done while the beans were buried underground beneath a fire or stored in a warm place in the house, for example under the kotatsu.

Regardless of the process, Japanese manufacturers need permission from the prefectural government, as required by food sanitation law. Most of the Natto on sale is made using B. subtillus natto as a seed germ that is cultivated in a pure culture.

All right, now that all the technical stuff is out-of-the-way, how is Natto eaten? As I said before, it comes with soy sauce and yellow mustard and is commonly eaten with white rice. Below are the step-by-step eating directions:

1. Open container.
2. Remove soy sauce and mustard pouches.
3. Remove plastic wrap cover and try not to inhale (well at least until you have eaten it several times and start to appreciate the finer qualities of its aroma).
4. Use chopsticks to stir the Natto (it will be in a hardish lump).
5. Don't get sick by looking at the long slimy mucus strings that drip off the Natto when stirring.
6. Add a raw quail egg (optional – well Sensei didn't make it optional my first time) and stir.
7. Add soy sauce and mustard. Stir.
8. Eat.

All joking aside, Natto is an acquired taste. I have never met anyone that liked it the first time they tried it. I'm not sure why I like it, maybe it is because Sensei said, "Samurai ate it all the time." or maybe because it is cool to like something that smells and looks so disgusting but I do like it. It should be noted however that eating Natto is a skill that isn't easily mastered. When you lift some Natto up to your mouth, there will be long slimy strings connecting your mouth to the Natto container. There is a very specific technique for getting rid of those with your chopsticks after the Natto is in your mouth. It is done by rapidly circling the chopsticks in small circles, half way between your mouth and the container, as if you were coiling up string.

So why eat it? Believe it or not, for the health benefits. Below is a list of proven and unproven claims about the medical benefits of eating Natto:

- According to Sensei, it is a common dish for monks in Japan and it helps with their meditation practice.
- Lowers Cholesterol.
- Prevents Obesity.
- The Japanese Navy used it to treat dysentery during WWII.
- It contains cancer-fighting chemicals. These are the same chemicals that are in tofu however.
- It contains large amounts of vitamin K2.
- Is currently being studied as a way to prevent Alzheimer's.
- It is generally accepted that consuming Natto reduces blood clots.
- And last but certainly not least, it causes men with hair loss to regrow their hair.

If you get a chance, give it a try. Just imagine you have walked all day, you have just removed your swords and have sat down for your first meal of the day. You remove a container filled with Natto out of your Kimono, along with your chopsticks. You open the container and start eating. Hopefully that imagery will help, because the smell will not.

Something to think about...

Image/Photo Citations

Photo 1:   Natto Mixed - Gleam - 11/01/2012
           http://en.wikipedia.org/wiki/File:Natto_mixed.jpg

Photo 2:   Natto Boxed - Toytoy - 11/01/2012
           http://en.wikipedia.org/wiki/File:Natto_boxed.jpg

Various pictures of Kanjuro Shibata Sensei XX

Umeboshi

I was first exposed to Umeboshi at Shibata Sensei XX's house in Boulder, Colorado. It was the day after I arrived at his home for one of my visits. He pulled out a fairly large container of round red wrinkled fruit looking things, opened it and offered me one. I put one in my mouth and almost spit it out. It was salty, sour and the texture wasn't that great. Sensei told me to eat more after I finished (with some effort) the first one. I declined. He then informed me that the Samurai use to eat them everyday. So I had another.

The next meal I was offered more and once again told about how "true" samurai would eat them all the time. It was almost as if I was being sold something by a very high-pressure sales person. So I asked Sensei why he was strongly "suggesting" that I eat so many of these, at the time, nasty things. He finally admitted that the Umeboshi I was eating were made in Japan by a family that was famous for producing very high quality and very expensive Umeboshi. It turns out that this family had given Sensei a large supply of them for when he was in the USA. That way he would never run out. It also turns out that Sensei had not eaten any of them and the family that gave him the full container was coming to visit in the near future. He was concerned that they would figure out that he had not even touched them and that was not acceptable to him. So the solution that he came up with was that I was to consume the entire contain full of Umeboshi before I left for home (5 days later).

I could tell that this really bothered him and I knew what I had to do. I had to consume over $500 in Umeboshi in 5 days. Yep, that's right, I was eating $100 of Umeboshi a day. By the time I was finished, I loved them. So what is an Umeboshi?

Umeboshi is a pickled ume fruit. Here in the USA people commonly call them "pickled Plums" which isn't really accurate. They are not plums. Umes are closer to what we call apricots.

Umeboshi is made by placing ripe ume fruit in a barrel with a large quantity of salt. The combination is slowly compressed to extract the juices from the fruit, which forms pickle brine. The salty brine is called Umezu and is used in many Japanese dishes as "vinegar". This process of compressing lasts around one month. The ume is then removed and sun-dried for about one week. Red Shiso (Akajiso) leaves are added to the brine, which turns it a bright red and acts as a preservative.

The ume is then added back into the brine/leaf mixture for five more days. This is what gives them their red color. They are then removed and placed in kegs to age for at least a year before being packaged and sold.

Umeboshi is commonly served with white rice. Typically one will be placed in the center of the rice so that the rice/Umeboshi combination looks like the Japanese Flag.

If you get a chance, give them a try. Just remember, it might require eating several before you come to "appreciate" them as I do.

Something to think about...

Image/Photo Citations

Photo 1: Umebosi Doyobosi – Naru-W – 11/01/2012
http://en.wikipedia.org/wiki/File:Umebosi_Doyobosi.jpg

Photo 2: Fruits of Japanese Plum – SEKIUCHI – 11/01/2012
http://en.wikipedia.org/wiki/File:Fruits_of_Japanese_plum.jpg

Photo 3: Makunouchi Bento – Kanko – 11/01/2012
http://en.wikipedia.org/wiki/File:Makunouchi_bento.jpg

Grandmaster Kyongwon Ahn teaching a Black Belt Class
(Pittsford, New York)

The Best Way to Get Rid of Pain after a Martial Art Class

The bruised, beaten, broken, aching, sore head, pain, so you can rest medicine.

As martial artists we inevitably get very sore and bruised muscles. Around twenty years ago, I was in a Tai Chi class and the instructor taught me a way to solve or at least diminish all of my martial art muscle pains. In this article I will pass this bit of knowledge onto you: a ginger bath.

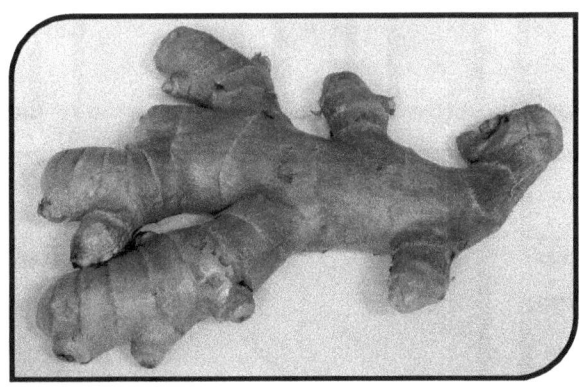

Take a fresh piece of ginger (dried ginger can be used but I prefer fresh ginger) and cut it up into very small slices or pieces, approximately 1 – 2 tablespoons. If this is the first time you have tried a ginger bath, use at most 1 tablespoon until you find out how your body reacts to the treatment. Place the ginger into boiling water and simmer for 15 minutes. While the ginger "Tea" is being brewed, fill a bathtub full of hot water (the hotter the better but don't burn yourself). Once the tea is finished, pour it into the bath. You might want to pour the "tea" through a strainer (I use a pasta strainer). Then take a bath. Don't use soap, just soak in the water for as long as you would like. Once you are done, dry off and then completely cover your body with fairly tight fitting comfortable clothing. In other words, wear a full set of pajamas or a soft cotton fleece top and pants, and socks. It is important that all the sore parts of the body are covered. You will then experience what can only be described as hot flashes. These will continue for quite some time. The ginger promotes blood circulation and therefore relieves sore muscles and decreases the amount of time a bruise will last. Repeat daily as necessary.

Something to think about...

Various pictures of Grandmaster Kyongwon Ahn

Self

Time Management – Why would anyone want to live like that?

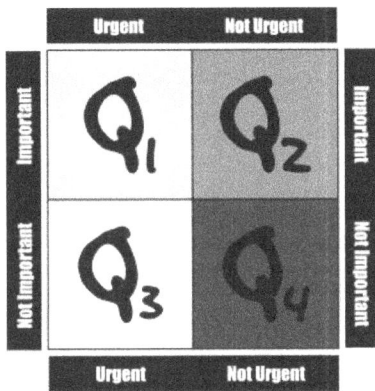

Last night I took a break from martial arts and played Diablo 3. Yes, I play video games occasionally. When I was playing, I noticed that a person I had played the game with a few days ago had already finished it and was almost finished playing through it a third time. The first thought that entered my mind was, "he's ahead of me" and I (for a very brief moment) wasn't happy. Then it hit me, why do I even care? I don't and I'm embarrassed that I did for even a second (or two).

In other articles, I've talked about time management skills and how people's lives can be drastically changed if they simply learn how to manage their time. I am a huge fan of Stephen Covey and when I teach time management classes I incorporate a lot of his ideas. In Covey's "7 Habits" book he introduced the concept of the 4 quadrants. Everything we do throughout the day can be placed into one of these quadrants. Quadrant 1 contains those things that are urgent and important. Quadrant 2 contains those things that are not urgent but are important. Quadrant 3 contains things that are urgent but not important. Finally, quadrant 4 contains things that are not urgent and not important. People that are able to primarily live in quadrant 2 are much more productive, efficient, have more free time and tend to be much happier due to a lack of stress caused by, "I don't have enough time in my day to do the things I want to do." People that live in quadrant 4 however live in the land of the living dead (I borrowed that expression from my wilderness survival training). They are not productive, not efficient, they might be happy but they contribute nothing to society and they could care less about bettering themselves.

I could spend an entire day lecturing on the 4 quadrants, so needless to say they are beyond the scope of this article. For this article I specifically want to talk about people who choose to live in quadrant four. Quadrant four, as I already stated, contains activities that are not urgent or important. I am totally dumbfounded at the number of people who spend most of their free time in this quadrant. I should point out that it is ok to spend some time there to unwind or simply do an activity you enjoy, because that might be something that you "need" mentally. "A break from reality", so to speak. But, think about it, if you need it, then it is important and falls in quadrant 2. The trick is knowing when you really don't "need" it anymore. After how much time of playing Diablo 3 do I personally shift out of quadrant 2 and into 4? Only I can answer that, but I need to be very honest with myself about what I truly need and not what I might just want.

Now I'm going to go off on a tangent (I tend to do that from time to time) for a second to talk about an average 9-5 person and his/her week. There are 168 hours in a week. A "typical" person works 5, 8 hour days for a total of 40 hours. That leaves 128 hours of non-work time. That is a lot of time. I know, "I have to sleep". Ok, if you go by what the doctors say, you need 8 hours of sleep a night (which by the way is ridiculous – I can get anyone down to 5 to 6 hours of sleep a night and they will be as rested as someone who sleeps 8 hours). That is 56 hours (or 35 hours) of sleep per week. That means that there are 72 hours (or 93) left in a typical person's week. You could work a second full-time job and have time left over. Think about how much you could get done, how many people you could help, how good of shape you could get in, if you applied all that time to doing activities in quadrant 2. I know what you are thinking, because I've heard it all before, you are thinking I have lots of stuff I have to do like chores around the house, shopping for food, taking the kids to soccer, etc. It's true there are a lot of activities that you have to do in your daily life that will take up a lot of your left over time. I bet however that you are spending a lot of time doing activities that are not urgent and not important: watching TV, playing video games, reading fiction, etc. How about this one, what do you do when you are driving? Do you listen to music? The drive itself might be important but listening to music isn't. Why not listen to an audio book, and not a fiction book. Here is a suggestion, listen to Covey's 7 Habits book. It changed my life. I can't tell you how many people comment to me on a regular basis, "how do you have time to do that?" I have time because I know how to manage my time, thanks in part to Covey.

Anyway, back to the article topic. We as a society need to get out of quadrant 4. I can't tell you how many students I have lost to activities in this quadrant. I guess it all comes down to what you want out of life. If you want to have "fun" and constantly feed the desire demon then live in quadrant 4. Chances are that if you are one of those people, you are not even reading this article because you are getting your quadrant 4 fix. However, if you want to improve yourself and through that improvement have a lasting beneficial impact on the people around you and society in general, then live in quadrant 2. So how do we do that? Constantly ask yourself, "What quadrant is what I am doing in?" If your answer is quadrant 4 (not urgent and not important), simply do something else.

If your answer is quadrant 3 (urgent but not important), ask yourself, "is it really urgent to me or just to someone else". Frequently people who are in quadrant 3 find themselves there because someone else thinks its urgent, when in reality it is not truly urgent for you. Regardless of the reason, finish up whatever you are doing in quadrant 3 (answering the phone, dealing with someone who walks into your office, etc.) and move out of that quadrant. It is possible, through some planning, to drastically cut down on the amount of time you are forced to spend time in quadrant 3. For example, I give all my statistics students my cell phone number so that they can call me when they need help. In the beginning they could call me at anytime (24/7). I found myself in quadrant 3 on a regular basis (sometimes at 2am). To partially get out of this quadrant, I set my phone so that it would only let calls, from my statistics students, through for a few hours each day. I cut my time in quadrant 3 down by 75% simply by making that change. Don't want people walking in your office without an appointment? Lock the door. I realize that some people, due to the nature of their work, can't make such drastic implementations but you can in your personal life. Turn your cell phone off. Turn your email program off. Believe it or not people were able to survive before cell phones and emails. With a little creative thinking anyone, no matter what their job or personal situation, can substantially cut back on the time spent in quadrant 3.

If your answer is quadrant 1, then at least you are doing something that is important, but why is it urgent? It is possible to have something come up that is urgent and important (a sick relative, an unexpected crisis at work, etc.) but a lot of times people find themselves in quadrant 1 instead of quadrant 2 because of procrastination. If there is a task in your future that is important, then get it done before it becomes urgent. That way you will be doing the task in quadrant 2 instead of 1. Why should we care? Where quadrant 4 is the land of the living dead, quadrant 1 is the land of stress and anxiety. Why would you want to live in either land? I wouldn't and don't. Make a conscious decision to live in quadrant 2, the land of productivity, creativity, and happiness and watch your life change almost immediately.

Something to think about...

Always seek Perfection or become Normal (aka one of the mindless masses)

$$E = Z_{\alpha/2} \cdot \frac{s}{\sqrt{n}}$$

$$E = 1.96 \cdot \frac{45.28}{\sqrt{50}} = 12.55$$

$$163.02 - 12.55 < \mu < 163.02 + 12.55$$

$$150.47 < \mu < 175.57$$

I teach statistics at a college level. This coming semester will mark the 80th time I have taught ECON221 - Statistics 1. I started teaching this class in 1994. Basically, I've been teaching it a lot for a long time. Over the years of teaching I have noticed something very disturbing, and very motivational. It is important to note that I have taught the same classes and used the same exams (well different numbers) for all those years. Back when I first started teaching, the mean (average) final grade for my students was normally in the mid 80's. Now it is in the mid 70's. What has changed? Well I curve my grades now and I didn't when I first started. I wrote a statistics textbook for my students so that they can understand the material better. Oh, and I give the students written procedures for how to solve every problem they will encounter in my class. I do all that just so my students can pass. In the beginning, there was no book, there were no procedures, there was no Internet, just overheads, and I really didn't know how to teach all that well. So what is going on? Why didn't the average go up?

> "Parents call it "bad grades", we call it "still passing."
> - Taken from a student's Twitter Feed

This is why. Nowadays, most students only care about passing and not about truly learning statistics. Ok, maybe not truly learning statistics but getting an "A" so that their GPA is as high as possible. I can't tell you how many students actually tell me, "as long as I get a 'C' I'll be happy", every semester. I never heard that 15 years ago. Instead, they would say, "anything but an 'A' is unacceptable to me", fairly consistently. Sadly, most of my students now only care about being average. That is what a "C" is after all.

I see this mentality everywhere. Instead of seeking perfection, which takes work, most people and companies seek normality. As I write this, I'm sitting in Starbucks looking out over an empty seating area. One of the employees just came out and "cleaned" the tables and chairs. Other than my wife and I there is only one person in here with us. In other words, there is nothing for the employees to do. So why are there food pieces all over the floor? Because that is where the employee, that was cleaning the tables, swept them. Sweeping the floor would take extra work. Why would he do that when he can get away with not doing it?

Why would anyone want to seek perfection when normality is accepted and expected? Because, if you strive for perfection you can and probably will achieve greatness or at least be elevated above the normal masses. Lets take a look at a company that never accepted "average", even when that would have been a huge improvement for them. This company started with two friends in a garage tinkering with electronics and grew into the highest valued company in the world. Steve Jobs never accepted normal or average, he demanded perfection of everyone that worked for Apple. If an employee didn't strive for perfection, they were out of a job.

I realize that achieving perfection might not be possible all the time, but it should always be strived for. Even if all my statistics students strived for a perfect grade and worked as hard as they could, not all of them would get an 'A'. But, I bet they would get higher grades than if they had just strived to pass the class.

So, what do you strive for? For me, anything but perfection from my Taekwondo students, the companies I deal with and myself is unacceptable. I admit there are a lot of things that I do that are not perfect but that is not due to a lack to trying on my part. It is due to my limitations, mentally or physically. What can I do then if these limitations prevent me from achieving perfection? Eliminate my limitations, that's what. For example, when I was a teenager, I was defiantly limited by that fact that I was ADHD. No, I was never diagnosed with this condition, but I could not control myself even though I tried. My instructor would tell me not to move when standing in line, but I would move anyway. I didn't want to but my body had other plans. This condition was limiting me and had to go. That is when I started meditating on a daily basis. Instead of sitting back and accepting my limitation, I utterly destroyed it.

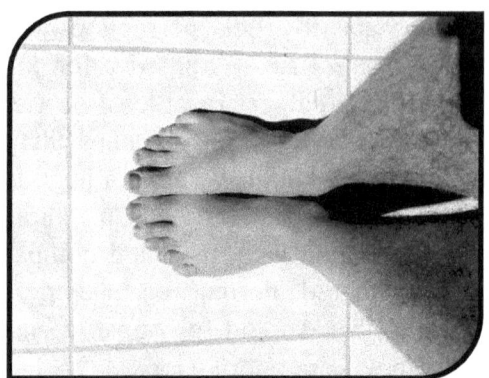
An almost perfect attention stance.

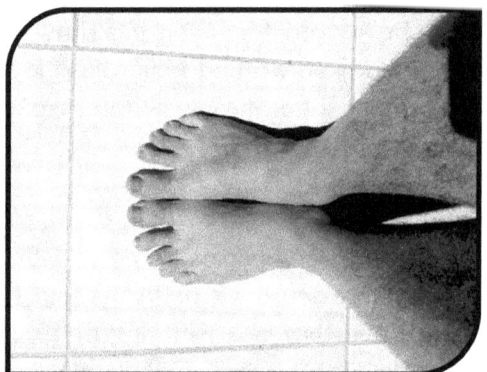
An average attention stance.

Always seek perfection or become normal (aka one of the mindless masses) and who wants to be normal?

Something to think about...

Get out of Your Rut and Slow Down Time

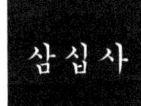

Once again winter is right around the corner. And, once again another year is about to come to an end. Sometimes, time just seems to fly by. You celebrate your birthday to only find yourself celebrating it again almost the next day. The older you get, the faster time seems to pass (well for most people). If you agree with everything I just said you are not alone but you are wasting your life away (well unless you want your life to be over).

Have you ever noticed that the first time you drive somewhere, it seems to take longer than the 100th time you make the same trip? I drive from Rochester, New York to Cincinnati, Ohio every few months and I have been doing that for 20 years (with time off here and there). The trip takes 8.5 hours. The first few times I drove it, it seemed to take forever. Over time the trip seemed shorter and shorter. Was it really shorter? No. The point is that my perception of the amount of time the trip took was less. So let's say that my trips only seem to take 5 hours each. If I live to be 90 and I continue to travel to Cincinnati until I die, I will have lost 450 hours of "time." That is almost 20 days. I bet when I'm taking my last breath that I will strongly desire to get those 20 days back. And that is only the "wasted" time from one part of my life. Imagine if I added up all the wasted "perceived" time. I bet that would amount to a year or more.

So why does this happen? Whenever we are in one of our life's many ruts we perceive the passage of time faster relative to when we are not in a rut. What is a rut? People tend to repeat what they are used to and not change. For example, do you always sleep on the same side of the bed? I bet the answer for most of you is yes. Why? The entire bed in the same, so why not sleep on the other side once in awhile? Oh I know, my alarm clock is on that side of the bed or my wife/husband sleeps on the other side. So what? What happens if you sleep somewhere else? Do the police come to arrest you? Try switching spots sometime and see how different the night is. Do you always drive the same way to work? Take a different route. Do you always eat the same food for breakfast? Do you always have the same Starbuck's coffee? If you drink Starbucks, try this, get a different coffee (it has to taste different) and observe how different the "perceived" time it takes you to drink it is compared to how long it takes to drink a regular coffee. Do you always go through the same morning routing to get ready for work? Every time you do something that is a repetitive process you are wasting "perceived" time. Don't live in ruts.

Here is a little homework. For just one day, before you do anything, ask yourself, "is this what I normally do?" If the answer is yes then do something else or do it differently. You will be surprised how much slower time goes by that day. Your day will seem like two days. I know there are some of you thinking, "I don't want my workday to go by slower." I bet when you are on your deathbed, if someone asked you if you would rather die or work several more days, you would pick the work. Have fun with this.

Something to think about...

Image/Photo Citations

Photo 1:   Greenwich Clock – Alvesgaspar – 11/01/2012
           http://en.wikipedia.org/wiki/File:Greenwich_clock.jpg

There are a lot of Different Types of People in this World – Now You can Group Them

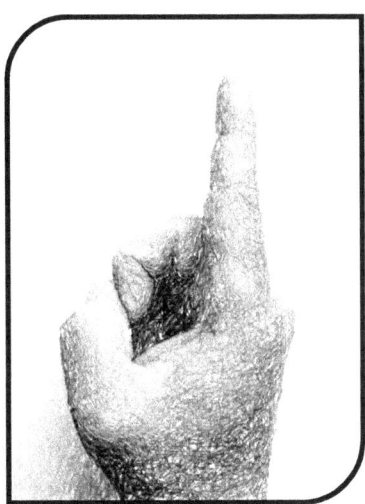

A couple of weeks ago I taught a Basic NLP Certification class at a local corporation. To go along with that class, I decided to compile a list containing some of the NLP groupings of people, which I copied out of the notes I took as an NLP student. Below are 5 of these groupings. Each grouping has categories contained within it. A person will tend to "default" to one of these categories. For example, Grouping #1: "To Be" or "To Have". A person will tend to fall into one of these categories most of the time. Is it possible for them to switch between the categories? Yes, but a person will tend to "default" into one. These are not by any means all of the groupings, but they are the ones I use the most. I have "classified" all of my black belts in all of these groupings so that I know how they think and will react to different situations. One classification is not better than the other, it's just who a person is and it gives me a little more insight into how they think. What type of person are you?

Grouping #1: "To Be" or "To Have"

"To Be"

- Will usually assume responsibility or blame themselves for problems or negative situations.
- This personality is caused by children having their needs excessively met. For example, when a child desires to be fed and is given more than needed or if a child needs warmth and more is given than needed.

"To Have"

- Will usually put the responsibility on others.
- This personality is caused by children's needs being inadequately met.

Grouping #2: "Pole", "Triangle" or "Circle"

Pole

- The Pole personality evolves from paternal influences. A Pole will be authoritative and know what they want. They will identify your problem but not solve it, or help you solve it. They will unconsciously display a pole symbol by pointing a finger, foot, pen, etc. and touch in a pole or pointing way.
- When resting face on hand, Poles will have their hand in a fist or simply rest their face on one finger or their index finger and thumb.

Triangle

- The Triangle is a helpful problem solver to the extent of doing things for you while attempting to help you. They can be helpful to the extent of smothering.
- Then resting face on hand, Triangles will completely open their hand and rest their face in it.

Circle

- The Circle is an ego personality. They will be reflective in nature. They will assist you with a problem by suggesting or offering a solution but not get directly involved in solving it. They will offer encouragement and follow up to make sure you came out ok, but they will not do it for you.
- Then resting face on hand, Circles will either bend their fingers at a right angle, with respect to their hand, and rest their face on the back of their fingers or they will rest their face on and open fist.

Grouping #3: "Blamer", "Placater", "Distractor" or "Computer"

Blamer

Words: Disagree – "You never do anything right."
Body: Blames – "I am the boss around here."
Insides: "I am lonely and unsuccessful."

- The Blamer is a fault-finder, a dictator, a boss. He acts superior and he seems to be saying, "If it weren't for you, everything would be all right." The internal feeling is one of tightness in the muscles and in the organs. Meanwhile the blood-pressure is increasing. The voice is hard, tight and often shrill and loud.
- When blaming, blamers breath in little tight spurts, or hold their breath altogether, because their throat muscles are so tight.
- Eyes bulge.
- Neck muscles and nostrils stand out.
- Face gets red.
- Voice sounds like shoveling coal.
- Face is screwed up.
- Lips curled.

Placater

Words: Agree – "Whatever you want is ok."
Body: Placates – "I am helpless."
Insides: "I feel like nothing; without him I am dead. I am worthless."

- The Placator always talks in an ingratiating way, trying to please, apologizing, and never disagreeing no matter what.
- He is a "Yes man."
- He talks as though he could do nothing for himself, he must always get someone to approve of him.
- Voice sounds whiney and squeaky.

Distracter

Words: Irrelevant – The words make no sense.
Body: Angular & off somewhere else.
Insides: "Nobody cares. There is no place for me."

- Whatever the distracter does or says is irrelevant to what anyone else is saying or doing, he never makes a response to the point. His internal feeling is one of dizziness. The voice can be sing-song, often out of tune with the words and can go up and down without reason because it is focused nowhere.
- He ignores everyone's questions; maybe even comes back with one of his own on a different subject.
- He might take an imaginary piece of lint off someone's garment.

Computer

Words: Ultra Reasonable
Body: Computers – "I'm calm, cool & collected.
Insides: "I feel vulnerable."

- The Computer is very correct, very reasonable with no semblance of any feeling showing. He is calm, cool and collected. He could be compared to an actual computer or a dictionary. The voice is a dry monotone and the words are likely to be abstract.
- Everything about a computer is motionless as possible, including their mouths.

Grouping #4: "Visual", "Auditory", or "Kinesthetic"

Visual

- **Body Posture:** Person leans back, with head and shoulders up or rounded. There is also a tendency to hold chin up.
- **Eyes:** These people might look up to their right or left, or their eyes may appear unfocused.
- **Gestures:** Their gestures are quick, angular and include pointing to eyes. Most are made above eye level.
- **Breathing & Speech:** High, shallow and quick.
- **Words:** The words that capture their attention include: see, look, imagine, perspective, reveal.
- **Presentations:** They prefer pictures, diagrams and movies.

Auditory

- **Body Posture:** Person leans forward, with the head cocked (as though listening), shoulders back & arms folded.
- **Eyes:** These people might look down to the left and may appear "shifty-eyed."
- **Gestures:** Their gestures are rhythmic, touching one's face, mouth and jaw (ie. Rubbing the chin). Most are made near ears or pointing toward the ears.

- **Breathing & Speech:** Mid-chest, rhythmic.
- **Words:** The words that capture their attention include: hear, listen, ask, tell, clicks, in-tune.
- **Presentations:** They prefer lists, summaries, quotes and things read to them.

Kinesthetic

- **Body Posture:** Person has head and shoulders down, with the body leaning slightly to the person's right.
- **Eyes:** These people might look down to the right.
- **Gestures:** Their gestures are rhythmic, touching chest. Most are below the chest.
- **Breathing & Speech:** Deep, slow with pauses.
- **Words:** The words that capture their attention include: feel, touch, grasp, catch on, contact.
- **Presentations:** They prefer hands-on, do-it demonstrations, test-drives.

Grouping #5: "Similar" or "Different"

"Similar" - people always compare how what they are doing is similar to something else.

"Different" - people always compare how what they are doing is different to something else.

Something to think about...

Worry – Who Needs It?

Every year, Native American Tribes from across North America converge on Halifax, Nova Scotia for the Annual Halifax Pow Wow. I had the privilege of attending it for two days. It reminded me of a martial art tournament in how the event was structured. I was truly amazed by the talent of not only the "dancers" but also the singers and drummers. I highly recommend it to anyone that has the ability to attend.

This Pow Wow got me thinking about the wilderness survival videos that I filmed over the course of the past four weeks, which in turn caused me to remember some of the survival classes I had taken personally. Quite a few years ago I was sitting in an old folding chair on a slab of ice. I was in the middle of the Pine Barrens, in New Jersey. It was nighttime, sometime in the beginning of February and I was listening to my wilderness survival instructor (Tom Brown Jr.) lecturing on the finer points of winter survival. I, along with the 50 other students, was freezing cold and there was no way to get warm until we went to bed (because we were in class), which wasn't for another 4 hours. After he was finished with his lecture, Tom said something that he had said before, but it really hit home that night. He said, "learning wilderness survival is like having insurance on your life. Just imagine, as you are driving down the road, you have the ability to pull over and walk out into the wilderness with only what you have on and live in a Garden of Eden." I started thinking about that and felt this huge weight lift off my shoulders. Think about it. What would you do if you lost your job, your home (because you lost your job and couldn't find work), your car, etc.? I would just walk out into the wilderness (probably the Adirondack Mountains) and survive as comfortably as I am now. True I wouldn't have my iPhone or my iMac or my iPad but instead I would have all the amazing things nature has to offer. Most people who interact with me on a daily basis see how connected I am to the modern world through my "toys" but I could easily give them up in a second. For example, the most exciting thing that I did today had nothing to do with modern technology, just the opposite; I spent a good amount of time petting a Raccoon (well in reality two raccoons until one of them tried to bite me).

Anyway, back to the Garden of Eden. I can't even begin to tell you how liberating it is to know I never have to worry about the things most people worry about. At any moment in my life, if things get out of control and are not looking good, I can simply walk out into the woods and never come back. Don't worry, I'm not going to do that, but the fact that I can, is very comforting.

So what does this have to do with martial arts? In a way we have a similar "life insurance policy." In this case it is being able to defend ourselves if we are ever attacked. I have had the "privilege" of being mugged twice in my life and I am still here. Not only am I here, I have a hard time even recalling all the specifics of the events because they were not that significant. I am not under the delusion that there is no one out there that could better me in a confrontation, but chances are they are not going to be mugging me. Most muggers out there are drunk, on drugs or simply don't know what they are doing. Please don't think I am trying to minimize the danger of being mugged because I am not. The first time I was mugged, a man wielding a broken beer bottle attacked me. If he had hit me with it, I could have been severely cut. Instead, I am saying that every martial artist has the tools necessary to help him or her defend themselves against a typical mugger. Are you guaranteed to win? No, but you have the ability to defend yourself to a far greater extent then someone who has no martial art training. Think about that and hopefully you will have a similar "dropping a heavy weight" experience as I did. You don't have to live in fear. This is a luxury most people don't have.

Something to think about...

Various Wilderness Survival Pictures

Grandmaster Gallano and Author Practicing Kali
(Toronto, Canada)

How to Manage Your Time

삼 십 칠

Students are always asking me how I have enough time in my day to practice Taekwondo (and the other art's I teach for that matter) and still have time to work and have a few minutes of free time. Normally, I answer that by simply telling the student to get a copy of (and read) Stephen Covey's book, "The Seven Habits of Highly Effective People." I don't follow the book to the letter but I do make use of a good portion of it. Most people fill their days with a lot of very small (and for the most part meaningless) tasks. Most of these might seem important but in reality are not. They don't even have an impact on a person completing the major goals they have set for themselves. What a student should do instead is focus on completing one or two tasks that will have a big impact on their goals and then fill in the rest of the day with the other tasks. That way they will have time to do almost anything they want. There is a story in Covey's book that does a great job of illustrating this:

> *A professor stood in front of a classroom full of students. He brought with him a large glass jar that he placed on a table, so that all the students could see it. He reached under the table and grabbed a bucket full of very large stones and poured them into the glass jar until it was filled up to the top. He then asked, "Is the jar full?" A student in the front of the class said, "Yes." The professor, instead of answering him, reached under the table and grabbed another bucket, this time filled with small*

stones. He poured them over the top of the large stones and shook the jar so that they filled all the empty space between the large stones. He then asked again, "Is the jar full?" Once again a student said, "Yes." He proceeded to grab a bucket filled with sand and pour it over the large and small stones. This time the sand filled the empty space between the stones. He then asked, "Is the jar full?" To that a student said, "No." The professor reached down and grabbed a bucket of water and poured it over the stones and sand, filling the jar to the top.

If the jar had been filled with the water first, there would have been no room for the stones. The water is the small insignificant tasks that fill up our day and the large stones are the tasks that are important and that will have a significant benefit to us if they are completed. So, add one or to large stones and a few small stones to each and every one of your days and then allow the sand and water to fill in the empty space. Don't fill your day with water.

"Ok, that sounds great, but how do you do that?" is normally what I get from students after telling that story. What I tell them to do is this (from Covey's book); List out all your current roles in life: Boyfriend, College Student, Taekwondo Student, etc. I then tell them to sit down Sunday night and ask themselves, "What one thing can I do this week that will have the most significant impact on each role?" Once those "things" are listed out, I tell them to write out what they have to do in order to successfully complete that task and when they are going to have it completed by.

Lets say one of my black belts has, Taekwondo as one of her roles. She decides that writing a post to her school's blog is going to have the largest positive impact on that role. So then she thinks about what she will need to complete that task. Luckily for her that only requires her to come up with a topic, actually write it and to post it to the blog. She might want to set of goal of writing it Thursday because she has a lot of free time that day.

That's it. Simply by identifying your roles and the tasks that will have the greatest positive impact on your roles, you will be able to get a lot more accomplished and still find time to do all the smaller insignificant tasks. So how can this system fail? Be careful of how big of tasks you pick for each role. For example, if the above black belt decided that her task was to learn the remaining 15 black belt forms that she doesn't know before the end of the week, she would fail. This failure only promotes failure in the future. Never set unattainable goals for yourself. Always start with small goals that you can constantly complete. This will improve your self-confidence in your ability to finish goals that you have set and will allow for larger goals to be set in the future.

It is truly amazing the number of goal/tasks you can complete in a week when following this system.

Something to think about...

Grandmaster Gallano and Author Practicing Kali
(Toronto, Canada)

Doctrine

The 8 Defilements

For this article I thought I would briefly discuss a topics that has recently come up in several conversations I have had with higher-ranking black belts. Most martial art schools have their students memorize and follow some sort of creed and my schools are no different. Below is the creed that we follow:

1. I resolve to cherish all life.
2. I resolve to tell the truth.
3. I resolve to respect my parents, teachers and elders.
4. I resolve not to speak of the faults of others, but to be understanding and sympathetic.
5. I resolve to overcome my shortcomings and not to praise myself or disparage others.
6. I resolve to practice tolerance and not to indulge in anger.
7. I resolve not to take what is not given, but to respect the things of others.
8. I resolve not to cause others to abuse alcohol or drugs, nor do so myself, but to keep my mind clear.
9. I resolve to remain in harmony with all the members of my family.
10. I resolve to always finish what I start.

We however look at our creed in a different light than most. Our creed is an indication as to the type of person a Taekwondo practitioner will turn into after years of practice. Indeed, a student should strive to live by the creed and, in accordance with the Doctrine of Behavior, take responsibility for their behavior relative to it by individually enforcing his/her own obligations through self-reprimands but it isn't a set of rules that must be enforced at all costs.

If our Creed is our Yang then our Um is our Defilements. Whereas the Creed is a list of qualities that we are striving toward, the Defilements are qualities we are trying to move away from. As a student begins their journey of Ten Thousand Miles within Taekwondo, they will inevitably exhibit all eight Defilements. However, as they progress though the years, the Defilements will start to subside and the Creed will start to manifest itself within them.

How many of these Defilements do you exhibit on a regular basis?

The Eight Defilements
여덟 더럽힘

흔
Excessive Happiness
(Hun)

불경기
Depression
(Bulgyeong-gi)

분노
Anger
(Bunno)

공포
Fear
(Gongpo)

걱정
Anxiety
(Geogjeong)

놀라움
Surprise
(Nollaum)

생각
Excessive Thinking
(Saeng-gag)

거만
Arrogance
(Geoman)

Something to think about...

Guidelines for Physical Development for Martial Artists

Ten Guidelines for Physical Development:

1. Respiration.
2. Verbal Expression of Exhalation.
3. Purposeful gaze.
4. Correct alignment of back and neck vertebrae resulting in proper balance.
5. Optimization of power achieved through correct hip motion.
6. Structural integrity of stances.
7. Interconnectedness and coordination of entire body.
8. Spatial awareness.
9. Proper alignment of the tailbone in relation to stance.
10. Connectedness to ground.

1. Respiration

Respiration is a very important part of a black belts training within Taekwondo. Without proper breathing, the body's mental and physical performance and control is decreased. My schools teaches eight different breathing methods: Abdominal Breathing, Replete Breathing, Yang Breathing, Yin Breathing, Square Breathing, Triangle Breathing, Bellows Breathing and Reverse Breathing.

2. Verbal Expression of Exhalation (Kihap)

The kihap serves two purposes within Taekwondo. The first purpose is that it forces the practitioner that is kihaping to exhale. When forcefully striking a heavy/unmovable target, it is very important that the breath not be held. If it is, the lungs can sustain damage in the form of ruptured alveoli. Therefore, if the practitioner makes it a habit of kihaping when striking a target, he/she will always be exhaling on impact, which will virtually eliminate the possibility of lung damage. The second purpose is that it helps focus the practitioner's mind on the impact with the target, which in turn increases the effectiveness of the impact. Within my schools there are three types of kihaps: two striking kihaps and a pushing kihap. When a kihap is executed during a strike, it either sounds like the practitioner is yelling "aaaaa" ("Eight" without the "t" on the end) or "eeeee". When a kihap is executed during a pushing technique/strike, it sounds like the practitioner is yelling "Oh". The kihaps, to a certain extent, actually sound like the strike/push they are executed with.

3. Purposeful gaze

While practicing Taekwondo it is always important for a black belt to know exactly where his/her eyes are looking and how he/she is looking. Most martial artists only focus on the "where" and not the "how". It is true that looking at your target is important, however that is not only what this guideline is concerned with. Instead, it is also concerned with how you look at a target/opponent. To get a feel for this "how", be mindful of people throughout the day that look at you and how they look at you. Some people will look nervous when looking at you, while others will look confident. Imagine the disadvantage you would have if your opponent can see hesitation, nervousness and doubt in your eyes before the actual confrontation. Now imagine the advantage you would have if the opposite were true. How you gaze can have a huge effect on a confrontation.

4. Correct alignment of back and neck vertebrae resulting in proper balance

The importance of keeping the back and neck correctly aligned for the technique, the stance, the jump, or the fall cannot be overstressed. As soon as the body/neck is out of alignment, the body will no longer be in correct balance. Because this alignment is different for different techniques, it is important that a student consult their instructor concerning how his/her back and neck should be held during the technique he/her is practicing.

5. Optimization of power achieved through correct hip motion

If you are in a car that is traveling 20mph and you throw a ball inside the car at 10 mph in the same direction as the car is traveling, how fast is the ball moving relative to the ground? 30mph. Without going into the physics of power and hip motion, simply think of it using the preceding example. If your kick is moving at 20mph with no hip motion, it will hit the target at 20mph. If your kick is moving at 20mph and your hip is moving at 10mph in the same direction, your foot will hit the target at 30mph. I'd rather have it hit at 30mph, wouldn't you?

6. Structural integrity of stances.

The structure of a student's stance is often neglected while focus is placed on other parts of a technique. The importance of a correct stance cannot be overstated. With a structurally correct stance there is more power in a technique, greater rootedness to the ground, greater balance, greater connectiveness between body parts and greater mobility. Once a stance's structure has been compromised, balance is lost, a practitioner is easily pushed over due to a lack of rootedness, the transition time into the next stance is increased and power is diminished. I can say for certain that everyone reading this (including myself) should spend more time on stance structure.

7. Interconnectedness and coordination of entire body.

In a lot of ways this guideline is very similar to the previous guideline. However, whereas guideline 6 is concerned about the static structure of the practitioner's body, this guideline focuses on the moving "structure" of the body. In other words, the efficiency of the pieces of the body while the entire body is in motion. As color belts, students' bodies tend to work against themselves. A student's hip might be moving clockwise when in reality it should be moving in just the opposite direction to interconnectively maintain moving structure and thereby increasing the coordination of the entire body. With practice and guidance from a knowledgeable instructor, a student's moving structure will gradually improve. That is why you see older masters being able to do physical techniques with greater outcomes than younger students. The younger students are stronger and more flexible but due to a lack of moving structure their bodies are not able to be as efficient as the older masters and therefore are not able to generate the same outcomes.

8. Spatial awareness.

Knowing exactly where different parts of your body are in relation to each other and where your body is relative to another person or inanimate object is very important. Imagine if you were attacked and went to block only to find out that you missed blocking the attacking limb. That mistake could cost you your life. Or, what if you were in a situation where you were required to defend yourself. You decided that you needed more space between yourself and your opponent, so you quickly moved backwards only to feel your head impact with a brick wall that was immediately behind you. Or, what if you are blocking with one arm and executing a strike with the other arm simultaneously. As both techniques are traveling toward the opponent, they hit each other because of a lack of spatial awareness, now the block didn't work and there was no strike. Increase is spatial awareness comes with time. It has been my experience that no matter how many or how few drills are practiced in an attempt to improve this ability, that the increase is dictated by the passage of time.

9. Proper alignment of the tailbone in relation to stance.

Believe it or not, the tailbone's alignment is a very important element of a correct executed stance. The general rule of thumb is that it should be pointed at a spot on the ground that is on the line that connects the practitioner's two feet. Its location on the line is determined by the ratio of weight on the practitioner's feet. For example, if each foot had 50% of the weight then the tailbone should be pointing to a spot on that line that is half way between the two feet. If on the other hand, 10% of the weight is on the front foot and 90% is on the back foot, the tailbone should be pointing at a spot on the line that is 10% of the distance of the line in front of the back foot. There are few exceptions to this rule. With proper alignment of the tailbone, balance is increased tremendously.

10. Connectedness to ground.

Being "rooted" or connected to the ground will provide a practitioner with greater power in his/her technique and will substantially increase the ability to defend against an attacker's throwing technique. This is easily observed when watching a small/younger student executing a jump side kick on a very heavy bag. When the student kicks, the bag doesn't move but the student goes flying back in the direction they came from. If, however, that same student executed a standing side kick on the heavy bag, the bag would move because the student's non-kicking leg was firmly rooted to the ground (if the technique was executed correctly). There was no root with the jump kick but there was with the standing kick. Same student, same technique, drastically different outcomes. Pay close attention to any weak points in the rooted foot/feet when executing a kick, strike or block. If they fail to maintain the root it will be blatantly obvious.

Something to think about...

Kanjuro Shibata XX Sensei
(Boulder, Colorado)

The Doctrine of Behavior
행 동 교 의

新虎館主義行為

Manners & Obligation

I would have to say that manners are one of the most important, if not the most important, mental aspect of Taekwondo. All of my schools follow a list of guidelines for both mental and physical development. Instructors, without a doubt, ask about one mental guideline more than any of the others: "Dispelling all negative thoughts and preventing future ones by self-reprimand." This guideline is one of the more difficult to follow because only the practitioner knows if they are truly following it. This way of taking responsibility for one's thoughts should carry over into one's physical actions as well, within Taekwondo practice as well as everyday life. I constantly see color belts forget to do something, like bowing onto the training floor, that they should have done and immediately look around to see if any of the black belts saw them forget. If no one saw them, they get a "phew" look on their face and continue as if they did nothing wrong. Ideally, a student should realize that they didn't do something, which they were supposed to do, and reprimand himself or herself through either a mental or physical self-reprimand. This practice is part of the Doctrine of Behavior.

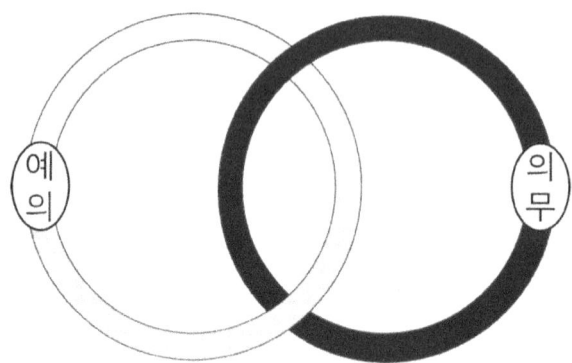

The purpose of this doctrine is to help students recognize and take responsibility for their own behavior and development both as martial artists and human beings. Essentially, the Doctrine of Behavior operates under the principle that when an individual enforces his own obligations; in other words, self-reprimands in the case of a breech of conduct, the lesson is more deeply learned than when obligation is applied by an instructor or other authority. In the case of a violation of the code of conduct, general martial arts (or common) etiquette (manners), or otherwise pre-determined rules of behavior both inside or outside the Dojang, the offender should impose a reprimand upon himself, within his school's guidelines, until he feels that he has met the obligation. Only a senior can tell an individual that he has such obligation but ideally the individual should begin to realize this on his own. In the case that the individual who committed an offense goes beyond what can said to be requisite (or nears a physically or mentally dangerous level of reprimand) a senior can and should intervene and release the individual of his obligation. The opposite is also true – the senior may insist that the obligation was not adequately met and require the offender to repeat or revise the reprimand.

A good way of understanding this is to imagine that you have two large cups. One cup is your "manners" cup and the other cup is your "obligation" cup. Your "manners" cup is completely full when you start Taekwondo and in the case of a perfect martial artist, it will remain that way. However, none of us are perfect so, whenever you do something that isn't correct manners (etiquette) some of the liquid in your "manners" cup is transferred to your "obligation" cup. That liquid must be moved back to the "manners" cup as soon as possible and this is achieved through reprimand (think of it as a liquid pump). The more and/or greater the reprimand, the more liquid is moved. Once the "obligation" cup is empty, the reprimand can stop. As I stated above, normally the student that has the obligation determines this but if a senior feels that the obligation has not been met, the reprimand can be lengthened or increased.

Through a commitment to the Doctrine of Behavior, both students and instructors can better themselves not only as martial artists but also as a global citizen.

Something to think about...

Various old Pictures of the Author

Kanjuro Shibata XX Sensei
(Boulder, Colorado)

Taekwondo

Taekwondo is more than just Kicking and Punching or "Wait, really, my belt has two ends?"

As a teenager, the simple act of walking out onto the training floor was always a challenge for me. It was a very rare day that I didn't do something wrong the instant my foot hit the floor, which inevitably resulted in me doing pushups. "What could I possibly do wrong?" you ask. Well let's see, there was the occasional forgotten bow, there was my lack of awareness of my instructor standing next to the door, which resulted in me not saying, "Hello Sir", there was even the one time my foot caught on the edge of the mat and I fell flat on my face at the feet of my instructor. The list goes on and on and on...... One day, I was so excited when I realized that I was at least 10 feet out onto the training floor and I wasn't doing pushups. I looked around the room with a big smile on my face, as if I had just won some major award. That is when I saw my instructor walking toward me and my smile instantly faded. I thought, "Pushups! You are smiling," but alas no. Instead, he walked over to me and gently took the ends of my belt in his hands. He then pulled them straight out in front of my body to illustrate that one end of my belt was longer than the other. Then he asked, "Are you physically deficient or mentally deficient today?" and then walked away. He later explained that the ends of the belt represent the mental and physical aspects of Taekwondo and that like a correctly tied belt, with equal length ends, they should both be practiced equally.

Unfortunately, very very few schools teach Taekwondo that way and I'm sad to say my instructor at that time didn't either, for the most part (there was a reason for that). Please don't think for a second that I am in any way putting my instructor, at that time, down because I'm not. I owe everything to him and if any aspect of his teaching was changed I might have never made it to where I am today. He as a student, like most Taekwondo students, was never taught anything but the physical aspects of Taekwondo. Sure, he learned the basic history of Taekwondo, some Korean terminology, manners, the creed, etc. but that is where it stopped. And, because of his limited exposure to the mental aspects, he was not able to expose his students to anything more than what he had learned.

If someone comes up to you and whispers the truth to you in your right ear and someone comes up to you and asks for the truth out of your left ear, you have an obligation to share that truth!

I recite that quote to my students more than I'm sure they would like but it is very important in respect to this article. Almost everyone that hears it assumes I am stressing the need to teach (share the truth) and they would be right, but in this case I'm not. In this case, I would like to focus on the fact that the quote illustrates that we can only pass on that which has been passed on to us. So my instructor was doing exactly what he should have been doing, passing on what was passed on to him. His instructor was doing exactly what he should have been doing, passing on what was passed on to him. As long as the "passing on" is 100%, no one was doing anything wrong. Therein lies the problem.

"Back in the day" students would attend class every day and instructors would have a lot more time to teach both the mental and physical aspects of Taekwondo. Nowadays, for most schools, that isn't possible. Nationally, most students on average attend classes twice a week for 60 minutes. So most instructors that have the knowledge to teach the mental aspects of Taekwondo, out of necessity, have opted to focus on the physical aspects. This selective focus has forced the shift of Taekwondo from a Martial Art to a sport or simply a physical activity. OK, before everyone reading this gets all bent out of shape, I realize that this isn't true for every Taekwondo school but it is for most. Even my school isn't immune to this shift. I simply don't have enough classroom time to pass on everything I know. I too am forced to spend most classroom time teaching physical techniques. Over 20 years ago, in an effort to help balance this lack of teaching the mental aspects, I started offering a "Winter Retreat". This annual retreat exclusively offers the students access to the mental side of Taekwondo. However, even that isn't enough because the material covered at the retreat is almost never repeated once taught. There simply still isn't enough time.

So, what is the solution? Most instructors would say, "students need to learn the mental aspects of Taekwondo off the training floor, on their own." Back in 1990, Grandmaster Ahn and I had this very discussion. I brought up that fact that we needed to teach more of the mental aspects and he promptly asked, "When?" He talked about how there simply isn't enough time in class and if he made time, the students would end up failing their physical promotion exams. He felt, as I mentioned earlier, that it was the student's job to explore the mental aspects on their own time. I then pointed out my belief that most students don't do that. We went back and forth for almost an hour before he agreed to put his Black Belts to a test. Grandmaster Ahn came up with a list of topics he felt his black belts should have a working knowledge of. I then made up a written "quiz" based on that list. Grandmaster Ahn gave all the black belt that attended that week's black belt class the quiz and both of us were surprised by the results. I thought the grades would be lower than they were and he thought they would be higher than they were. After discussing the results, he came to the conclusion that students in general lacked mental knowledge do to a lack of easily accessible printed material and therefore the next week he called me into his office and tasked me with writing new manuals for his association.

Old United Taekwondo Association Manuals

That was the beginning of my obsession. Ask any of my students that have become Instructors, what I do in my spare time and they will all say, "Write Manuals!" Over the years, I have constantly rewritten and reworked the manuals until I finally was able to publish Shin Ho Kwan Volume 1 & 2 (300 pages), and I'm still not done. Currently I'm finishing up two new books on the mental aspects of Taekwondo. The first book that will be released is a collection of articles I have written over the years (this book) and the second book is on Do Meditation.

Enough about my books. So what is an instructor or student to do about all this? If you are a typical instructor and are only seeing your students 2 – 3 times a week, it is your job to make it as easy as possible for your students to learn the mental aspects. Here is a list of what I suggest:

- Write a manual for your school or use your association's manual or use another school's manual (with permission).
- Provide a reading list.
- Provide a movie (documentary) list.
- Have a school library.
- Give written exams.
- Start a blog that focuses on the mental aspects.
- Have a school web page (that contains material other than advertising).

- Host mental retreats.
- Host guest lecturers.
- Start a "club" within your school that focuses on only the mental aspects.
- And the most important of all, never stop learning yourself.

So what is a student to do about this? That's simple, constantly ask questions? There is nothing that upsets me more than a student that has one-on-one time with their instructor and they either don't talk or they talk about non-martial art related stuff. What a wasted opportunity! Believe me when I say you can never ask enough questions. Also, READ! How many books on martial arts have you read? How many books on Asian culture and philosophy have you read? With today's technology most of what was only available in book form when I was a color belt is available on the Internet for free, so there is no excuse for not reading something. If your school isn't providing you a balanced mental/physical education, you have two choices: learn it on your own or switch schools.

Something to think about...

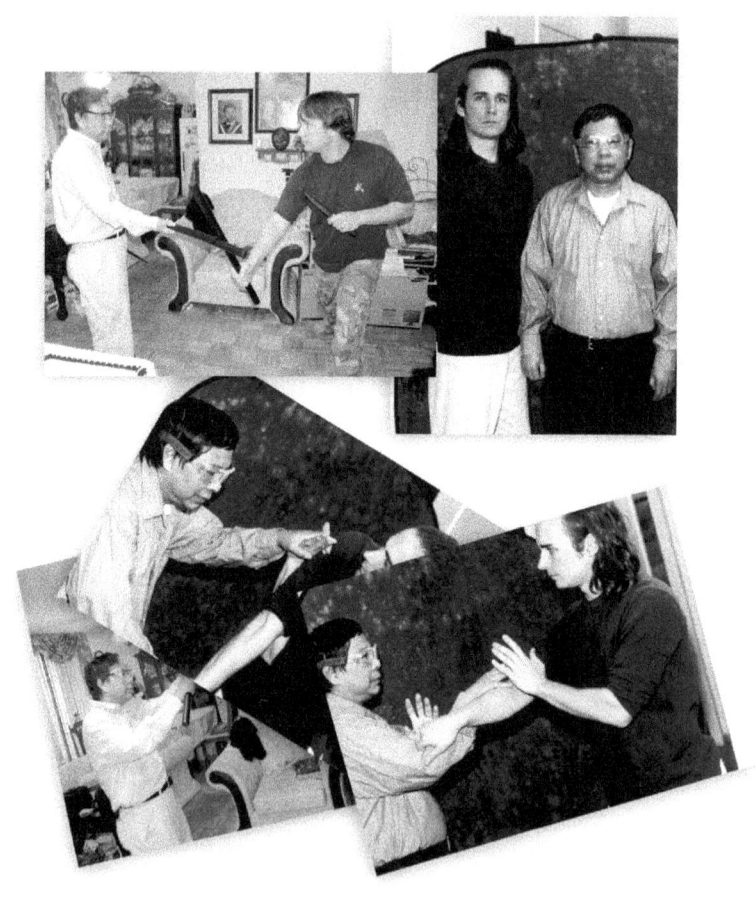

Grandmaster Gallano and Author Practicing Kali
(Toronto, Canada)

The Partial Art of Taekwondo

Last night I was sitting at a dinner table with a bunch of family members. Enjoying some of the best ribs I have ever had and some local freshly steamed muscles. It's truly amazing how cheap muscles are up here in Halifax. Anyway, toward the end of the meal the conversation switch to my travel plans for the rest of the summer. I told them (and now I'm telling all of you) that next Friday I will be traveling to Florida to board a 45' sailboat and to embark on a 7-day class. You see, I'm taking lessons on how to sail larger sailboats. It's the first part of a three-part class that will end with me sailing from St. Thomas to Bermuda to Road Island. After I was done explaining all about the sailing school, I told them that I would be returning to Halifax for a week and then I would be going to Rochester, New York to teach two weeks of Taekwondo Camp. To which my brother-in-law's wife said, "You know, I took the Partial Art of Taekwondo for 10 years." I thought I misheard her and said, "Wait, what did you say?" To that she replied, "I took the Partial Art of Taekwondo." At this point I can't tell you what happened because I don't want to be arrested.

Ok, not really but I was in shock. How could someone who actually took Taekwondo for any length of time say such a negative statement? It is not uncommon for people that have never taken Taekwondo to put it down but hearing a Black Belt in Taekwondo do that completely caught me off guard and led to me writing this article.

I really don't want to go into a detailed history of Taekwondo in this article, but it will be necessary to offer a brief overview. After WWII, martial arts started publicly being practiced in Korea again. What was being taught however was not a pure Korean martial art but a blending of traditional Korean martial arts (this is a topic for a future article) and various martial arts from Japan and China. These new arts were given names that ended with the word "Kwan" which loosely translated means "house of" (most people translate it as "institute"). After a number of years the heads of these Kwans got together and under the realization that a single martial art would be able to be spread globally better than a bunch of smaller ones, merged the Kwan's and formed Taekwondo (there is a lot of controversy surrounding the naming of Taekwondo but none of that is really important concerning this article). So what were all these Kwan heads to do? Each Kwan was a unique martial art. Each practiced a different set of forms, performed kicks and strikes differently, and in appearance might have been similar but in reality were different. They couldn't simply adopt one of the Kwan's curriculums. Can you imagine, "My Kwan is the best and we should use my curriculum!" What they did was create a new set of forms and standardize the way everything "Taekwondo" was done. They created "the World Taekwondo Federation" to govern Taekwondo and everything was good, or at least that is what everyone thought.

What these men did was truly amazing. I think anyone would be hard pressed to give an example of a group of very proud men getting together and agreeing on anything. However, what they did is also the reason why comments like "partial martial art" are frequently heard when referring to Taekwondo. They did create a new curriculum, but a lot of people would argue that is was only "partial." From my understanding it was their intention that this new curriculum would be "partial". It would be the fundamental core material taught at all Taekwondo schools and it would be supplemented with material from the school's Kwan. This however is not what, for the most part, happens in most schools nowadays. Instead, most schools have lost all connection to their founding Kwans and have therefore dropped most, if not all, of their Kwan's teachings. This leaves these schools with a very limited curriculum. There is nothing wrong with this however. There is a very successful chain of Taekwondo schools in my hometown that only teaches the core WTF curriculum. It focuses primarily on Olympic style sparring and is very successful at national level tournaments. They are very upfront about what they are teaching or rather how they are teaching Taekwondo. They are teaching a sport and they are very good at it. So how is what they do "partial"? It isn't, they are teaching a sport and their students (athletes) are taught by their instructors (coaches) everything needed to be successful in Taekwondo tournaments. Therefore, what they are learning is a complete system from the aspect of a sport.

Other schools have not abandoned their Kwan's curriculum and still teach everything from kicks to throws to pressure points to chokes to punches, etc. These schools are also "complete" because both the WTF curriculum and the Kwan's curriculum are taught and they are teaching Taekwondo as a martial art. So what Taekwondo schools are "partial" schools? They are the Tae Kwan Dough schools, the "McDonald" schools that pop up on every corner of larger cities and are constantly focused on how they can make more money. Now let me say there is nothing wrong with a martial art school being successful as long as their curriculum isn't dumbed down to facilitate that objective. Unfortunately, that is what a lot of schools have done. They removed all their Kwan's material not to focus on sparring competitions or some other aspect of the art but to allow students to successfully pass their promotion exams. The more promotion exams, the more money. The more promotion exams the more the students are happy because they are higher ranking. People love being praised and recognized. The boy scouts have it right with all the badges. Nothing inflates the ego more (and makes you feel better) than being higher than someone else. Students that feel good don't quit. Therefore, these schools have more students, which makes them more money, all by simply teaching half of what a "complete" martial art Taekwondo School would teach.

I remember I was giving a black belt promotion exam a long time ago. One of my female students was testing for 1st dan and she brought a friend to watch. This friend was taking Taekwondo at one of the local "McDonald" schools. She loved her school and was very proud of her master instructor. My student would constantly tell her to transfer to my school so they could practice together. Her friend would try to get my student to leave for her school. Needless to say, neither one switched. They spent a lot of time together outside of Taekwondo but never visited each other's schools until they tested for their black belts. The friend tested first and successfully passed her test. She then came, a few months later, and watched my student test (who also passed). After the exam she came up to me and said, "I am so embarrassed." I then asked, "About what?" She then explained that she was a black belt and never learned a quarter of the material she just saw her friend do on her promotion exam. I told her she had nothing to be embarrassed about, that each Taekwondo school was different and that she should be proud of herself. About a month later she stopped taking Taekwondo.

This all boils down to one question: what do you, the Taekwondo student, want out of Taekwondo (and not what anyone else wants)? Do you want to compete in tournaments? If so, the school you are attending is "partial" if it doesn't provide you the means to achieve your goal. Do you want to simply take Taekwondo to get in better shape? A school that focuses on the workout aspect of Taekwondo is for you. Be brutally honest on what you want or you might just find yourself in ten years saying, "I'm so embarrassed."

Something to think about...

Who Wants to Learn Magic?

사 십 삼

A couple of days ago I went to the last Harry Potter movie. Let's get this out-of-the-way now – I am a Harry Potter fan. I arrived over an hour early because I thought, "I'll get there early, before everyone else so I can get a good seat." Well, it turns out that everyone else decided to get there an hour and a half before the movie and I was therefore last in line. I did manage to get a good seat however. After the initial excitement of getting a good seat wore off, I realized that I had over 45 minutes to wait for the movie to start. I immediately thought, "I'll just meditate" but alas whenever I do that people tend to stare. I have tried several ways of meditating in the past that I thought no one would notice but it never fails, after about 15 minutes the fingers start pointing. Basically, anyone that sits for over 15 minutes without moving starts to attract attention. I think next time I'll lean my head back, open my mouth, close my eyes, and start working on one of the more challenging koans. Hopefully everyone will think I'm just sleeping. Nothing odd about a middle-aged American male taking a nap at a movie theater due to a lack of sleep caused by working an 80 hour week, sitting in front of the computer for hours on end and almost never sleeping. Yet I digress.

There I was sitting and waiting. In order to pass the time a little faster I starting listening to the conversations the people around me were having. As was to be expected, they were all concerning Harry Potter. One ended up catching my attention more than the others. The two young males were talking about how much they wished Hogwarts really existed and that they both wanted more than anything to be able to attend that school to study magic. They talked about how they would practice endlessly until they were able to perfectly cast all the more difficult spells. They talked about how they would spend hour upon hour in the library reading all the books about magic. On and on they went until they finally concluded they would become the best wizards Hogwarts had ever seen.

I felt like saying to them, "Instead of talking about it, why don't you just go do it?" To which they would say, "How can we? Hogwarts doesn't exist." It is true that the fictional school in the Harry Potter books doesn't exist, but there are thousands of schools across the US that do teach magic. They are martial art schools. I know what is going through your minds, "that's not the same." I would have to disagree and say that anyone that would say that is speaking out of ignorance. Almost every spell has a martial art counterpart. It might take on a slightly different form but in the end it will achieve the same result. If what we do isn't magic I don't know what is. We can control a person both physically and mentally with little effort. We can destroy boards, bricks, stones, etc. with our hands and feet. We can heal the injured. We can sense someone's intention to move before they actually move. We can withstand extreme temperatures, both hot and cold. We can endure a very high level of pain. We can control our breathing to alter our mental state. The list goes on and on and on. The point is, if you don't have to ability to perform magical feats, practice more. Remember it took Harry almost an entire school year to be able to successfully cast the Patronus spell.

Something to think about...

Pictures from a 1992 Promotion Exam

The Martial Artist "Type"

For this article I thought I would talk about a somewhat more advanced topic: the martial artist type. Within my Taekwondo school we practice the Taegeuk Forms as color belts. There are eight of these forms and each one is based on one of the eight trigrams. Without going into a lot of detail, trigrams are a series of solid and broken bars that are arranged in three bar combinations. The bars that make them up are representations of Um (broken line) and Yang (solid line). The order in which the bars are arranged within the trigram gives it specific characteristics. Each trigram has numerous attributes, ranging from an elemental manifestation, to a direction, and to a familial relationship. Most people have the easiest time conceptualizing the true essence of a trigram when generalizing them with simply the corresponding element, so that's what I will do for the rest of this article.

The eight elemental manifestations that correspond to the trigrams are: heaven, lake, fire, thunder, wind, water, mountain and earth. Everything in the world, from a physical object, to a school of thought, to a movement, etc. can be classified into one of these eight categories. This includes us as martial artists. Every Taekwondo practitioner, individually, tends to default to an individual one of these categories. So what determines what trigram a person is? Everything from body type to personality. For example, martial artists that fall into the earth or mountain trigram category tend to have large muscular bodies. Whereas, martial artists that fall into the thunder or wind trigram category tend to have wiry bodies. However these generalities are not always the case because of all the other factors that go into classifying an individual. I once practiced with a huge short male student that definitely fell into the wind trigram. This totally went against the "body type" standard. In order to correctly classify a martial artist, everything must be taken into account: body type, mind (how they act), how they move, how they interact with other people and the environment, how they talk (speed and volume), etc. It is not easy to classify someone and it takes years of observing various martial artists from all eight categories in order to be any good at it. To make matters worse, it is also possible for someone to change from one category to another as they progress along their martial art path, which means once a classification has been made that it could be incorrect in a very short period of time.

For a martial artist that doesn't have access to someone that can correctly classify them, there is a tool that can be used to get fairly accurate results: the Taegeuk forms. Simply watch someone do all the Taegeuk forms and take note of which form looks the closest to the element it represents. One should really stand out, or at least two forms that are relatively close to each other (mountain and earth for example). Once you believe you have found the "one" that the person falls into, watch them do the Taegeuk forms again. You should be able to see a little bit of that element in every form.

So why is it important? Because, once you understand what Trigram you represent, you can immediately take advantage of that Trigram's strengths and know of its weaknesses. You can also, with a lot of practice, switch into a different Trigram when necessary. Looking at an example might help with the understanding of this somewhat difficult concept. I fall into the "water" trigram. I haven't always, but I have been firmly rooted in it for the past 10 or so years. If I was to enter into a standing grappling match with another martial artist, assuming our physical abilities were closely matched, what Trigram would that person have to fall into in order to never be able to defeat me? If you answered "fire" you would be correct. Fire and water completely negate each other, neither one having the advantage. Both of us would look for openings in each other but we would never find them. Neither one of us would ever be victorious unless fatigue overtook one of us. You might be saying, what's the point then? Why would I ever enter into a match with someone that I could never beat? Because, I can't lose. A Demosthenes quote comes to mind, "he who fights and runs away, lives to fight another day." The "another day" in this case isn't truly another day but a period of time in the match that I decide on. When the match starts we (my opponent and I) are in complete balance. I don't have to worry about being defeated, instead I can focus on what "trigram" I will switch into in order to defeat my opponent. Then, when the moment is right, I will make the switch and be victorious.

I know what you are thinking, "what prevents your opponent from doing that?" Nothing, but it isn't very common. Let's say for example, it did happen in my match. I would simply change as soon as I noticed the change in my opponent. This change would not last long and we would then both be back to our original default trigrams. Hopefully I would eventually be able to make a change without my opponent being able to counter it. If not, the changing back and forth would last until one of us successfully made the change without the other following or one of us was defeated due to fatigue.

Side Note: It is important to remember that all of this is only relevant with equally matched opponents. If one opponent is drastically superior to the other, the trigram grouping is of no consequence.

Initially this "trigram negation" method is most easily applied in a grappling setting (either standing or ground) but with some practice it can be used in free sparring. In fact everything we do in Taekwondo can benefit from being able to switch from one trigram to another. Certain trigrams are better for certain types of breaks. Just think how much better your Taegeuk forms would look if you could change your trigram to correspond to the trigram of the form with no "hint" of your default trigram.

I don't want to go into any more detail about this subject. It is important to experiment (play) with this concept on our own. You will learn a lot more and it will have a much bigger impact on you than if you are simply spoon-fed the knowledge.

On a side note: This way of learning applies to a lot of material within martial arts. One of my black belts said to me after a retreat, "why have you never taught this to me before?" Why? Because if she had figured it out on her own, she would never have forgotten it. That is truly the best way to learn.

I'll leave you with one last thought: remember everything can be grouped into one of these trigrams, that includes weapons. You should use a weapon that is in the same trigram as you are. Hopefully that will make you even more frustrated.

Something to think about...

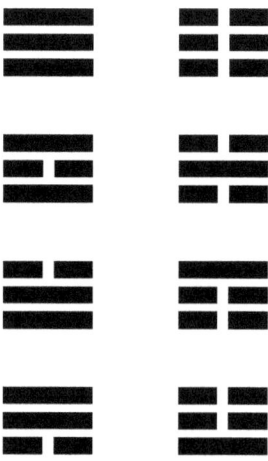

I accept it with an Open Heart

Bodhidharma once said:

In countless ages gone by, I've turned from the essential to the trivial and wandered through all manner of existence, often angry without cause and guilty of numberless transgressions. Now, though I do no wrong, I'm punished by my past. Neither gods nor men can foresee when an evil deed will bear its fruit. I accept it with an open heart and without complaint of injustice.

This was the advice that he gave his "students" when they encountered adversity in their training.

When I first entered into a live-in Taekwondo program, I took a copy of that quote and hung it in a place that I could read it everyday (or whenever I needed to). It is true that Bodhidharma directed the above advice to people following what would become the Zen Buddhist tradition, but it could just as easily have been given to anyone that has ever practiced a martial art.

As martial artists we also wonder through all manner of existences. We travel from the role of a student to the role of a master instructor. We start, knowing nothing of our art (way). Eventually we end up knowing something but once we think we do, we in fact have traveled back to the beginning, because that which we think we know isn't really that which can be known. We are constantly fighting ego and if we are not, the ego has already won. We experience emotions we didn't even know we had: joy, happiness, sadness, anger, etc. One second we are bowing to someone that we are learning from, while the next second someone is bowing to us because we are teaching him or her. It is always a battle between the student and instructor within us and the instructor only wins when the student wins. The best way to tell a great instructor is to watch them as a student. If they are not a great student, they are not a great instructor. So many black belts lose sight of the fact that we are all still students and will always be. The moment we think we are not a student is the moment that we cease to be a martial artist.

As students we constantly face the challenges of being a student. A good instructor will put us in situations to test our resolve, to check our egos and to see if we truly can accept our training with an open heart and without complaint of injustice. Because if we cannot, we fail as a student and as an instructor.

I constantly ask my students to do things that they will not like, I have them repeat techniques to the point of complete exhaustion, I test their resolve to be martial artists and I utterly crush their egos. At the same time, I am forced to do things I don't like, I have to repeat techniques to the point of complete exhaustion, my resolve to be a martial artist is tested and hopefully my ego will someday be crushed. I, like my students, enter into classes as both the student and the instructor. Success is determined by if we all leave as we started our training – as students, as beginners, as white belts.

Something to think about...

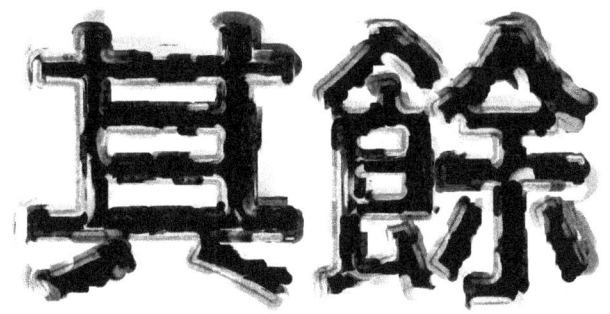

Others

My First Taekwondo Winter Retreat

Back in 1990-1991, Grandmaster Ahn gave everyone that came to class one night a surprise written exam on the mental aspects of Taekwondo. This exam was an eye opener for most of the black belts that took it. Needless to say, there were a lot of bad grades and it was obvious that more attention needed to be placed on the various mental components of Taekwondo. This really motivated me to learn more and started me down a new path of study. My first area of exploration was the Trigram and the Taegeuk Forms. I spent a lot of time asking questions and reading about them. Once I had a general understanding of the Trigrams and their relationship to the forms, I wrote an article for Taekwondo Times. This was just the beginning of my new obsession.

Once I moved back to Rochester in 1992 after working with Grandmaster Ahn is Cincinnati for two years, I started teaching Taekwondo at several local YMCAs. A group of black belts that had been with me before I moved to Cincinnati started coming to my classes again. I had a fairly large number of students within a very short time and I knew that I had to place a strong emphasis on the mental aspects of Taekwondo, especially when teaching my black belts. I wanted to share my love for this knowledge with them. The problem was figuring out a way to do that without them all dropping out. I was convinced that if I devoted a lot of class time to anything other than physical techniques that I would have students leaving or at least complaining. That is when I came up with the idea to have a winter retreat. The retreat would solely focus on everything in Taekwondo that was not physical. I knew that the local YMCA had a camp up in the mountains that they rented to snowmobilers in the winter. I thought that would be perfect, because it would be in the middle of nowhere and there wouldn't be any of the daily distraction. After sending out flyers to my black belts, I was truly amazed that all of them signed up for the 3-day retreat. "All of them" was only 5 at the time: Master VanHee, Master Humble, Mr. Smith, Mr. Folks, and Mr. Berry.

Because my experiences with these sort of events were all in the form of very strict Japanese meditation retreats, that I had attended frequently, I think I might have overdone it the first year. We all arrived Friday afternoon and I immediately started teaching classes on various Chi Kung exercises. These exercises consisted of holding the arms in different positions for a very long time while doing various breathing techniques. By the end of the night the black belts were in a lot of pain and ready for bed. Bed consisted of very old dirty bunk beds that none of us could really fit into. They did provide entertainment however, because there was writing all over them and the walls. The summer campers had a lot of interesting things to say.

At 4:30 in the morning I rang the wake up bell. Mr. Smith jumped so high when I rang it that he hit his head (having slept on the top bunk) on the ceiling so hard that I thought he knocked himself out, but all he did was create a lump the size of an egg. At that point everyone had 15 minutes to get ready for walking meditation. Walking meditation was outside and lasted 15 minutes. While walking, a group of snowmobilers was returning back to their cabin after having consumed a large quantity of alcohol at a local bar. They slowed way down as they passed us and I'm not sure if they believed what they saw was real or was caused by the beer. We couldn't see their faces but all their heads turned as they went by.

After walking meditation was finished, we returned to the cabin to start seated meditation. This lasted for 6 hours, with only a 30-minute break for breakfast. I had decided that Saturday from the bell until 4 in the afternoon was going to be silent and that there would be no talking under any circumstances. Well, I had to talk to teach the classes that were held after meditation but I tried to minimize this as much as possible. Lunch came and went and so did another class or two. Around 2pm I gave them a break in order to take showers. The cabin didn't have any showers, so off they went to a building that housed all the showers for the camp. Once they entered the building, several of the snowmobilers saw them and started asking them question about what my black belts were doing outside at 5am. The problem was that the black belts couldn't answer due to my rule on not speaking. They tried to use hand gestures to communicate that they could not talk but it was a disaster, so they gave up and stayed to themselves. At 4pm when they could finally talk, they really didn't say that much. They acted like they were drugged. I felt like I had to do something and I decided that this "state" could easily be cured by a nice walk through the woods. So we all jumped into a couple of cars and drove down the road to a parking lot at the beginning of a hiking trail, and off we went. Well, until a cross-country skier got upset with us for destroying the snow on the trail. So, what were we to do? I looked around and saw a nearby mountain and decided that the best course of action was to climb it. That climb has become a tradition and we have climbed it every year since then.

Once back in the cabin, it was time for dinner. Then I taught several classes on Iron Shirt Chi Kung, after which it was time for bed. I had decided that I wanted to teach them all a lesson on how much the mind can affect our perception of how sleepy we are, so I rang the bell at 2am instead of 4:30am. There were no clocks allowed at the retreat so there was no way for them to know what time it really was. The morning was identical to the previous day. Walking meditation followed by seated meditation. We only sat for a couple of hours however. Then I told them they could all talk because I wanted to ask them a few questions. I asked them how sleepy they were that day compared to the previous day. How difficult it was to get up and how their meditation went. They all felt that it was easier than the day before. No one had any clue that it was only 4:30ish when they were answering my questions. Even after I told them, a couple of them didn't believe it. It was amazing how sleepy they all got once they really knew the time, so I let them go back to bed.

That was all I really remember about the first Winter Retreat I taught. We have come a long way. A few years ago we had over 50 adult black belts at the winter retreat from 4 states and two countries.. It is amazing how far we have come.

Something to think about...

Pictures from the 2008 Winter Retreat
(Adirondack Mountains, New York)

Pictures from the 2012 Winter Retreat
(Adirondack Mountains, New York)

Affirming Faith in Mind – Translation by Ormond McGill

In this article I thought I would share a translation of the Shinhinmei (Verses of the Believing Mind) by Ormond McGill. Mr. McGill, even though I have only taken a handful of classes from him, had a big impact on me through his writings (and translations).

> *The Way comes most readily for those who have few preferences. When wishing for and wishing against are both absent, everything becomes clear and undisguised. Make distinctions, however, and heaven and earth are set far apart. If you wish to see the truth, then hold no opinions for or against anything. To set up what you like against what you dislike is the disease of the mind. When the deep meaning of things is not understood, the mind's essential peace is disturbed.*

> *The Way is perfect like vast space, where nothing is lacking and nothing is in excess. Indeed, it is due to our choosing to accept or reject that we do not see the true nature of things. Live neither in the entanglements of outer things, nor in one's inner feelings. Just be serene in the oneness of things and such*

erroneous views will disappear by themselves. When you try to stop activity to achieve passivity, your very efforts fill you with activity. As long as you remain in one extreme or the other, you will never know oneness.

Those who do not live in the Way fail in both activity and passivity. To deny the reality of things is to miss their reality, just as to assert the purposelessness of things is likewise to miss their reality. The more you talk and think about it, the further astray you can wander from the truth. It has been said by many masters that if one stops talking and thinking, there is nothing you will not be able to know. At the moment of inner understanding, there is a going beyond that which appears to be and that which appears not to be. Thus, do not search for the truth; only cease to cherish opinions.

Do not exist in a dualistic state, for if there is even a trace of this and that, of right and wrong, the mind will be lost in confusion. At their roots, all dualities come from a single source, which we can call the One ... but do not become attached even to this One. When the mind is undisturbed as to which way it should choose, but just allows what IS to be, there is nothing in the world, which can offend. And when a thing can no longer offend, it ceases to exist with the strength it had. To live in the Way is neither easy nor difficult, but those with limited views are fearful and irresolute, and the faster they hurry the slower they go, and clinging cannot be limited; even to be attached to the idea of the Way is to go astray. Just let things be in their own way, and there will be neither coming nor going.

Obey your natural nature and you will walk freely and undisturbed. When thought is in bondage, the truth is hidden, for everything is murky and unclear, and the burdensome practice of judging brings annoyance and weariness as no benefits can be derived from distinctions and separations.

If you wish to move in the Way, do not dislike the world of senses and ideas. Indeed, to accept them fully is identical with the true Way. The wise strive for no goals; only the foolish fetter themselves. Distinctions arise from the clinging needs of the ignorant. To seek the Way with a discriminating mind is the greatest of all mistakes.

For the unified mind in accord with that which IS, all self-centered striving ceases. Doubts and irresolutions vanish, and the real fullness of living is possible. When all is empty, clear, and illuminated with no exertion of the mind's power, we are freed from bondage. For in this world of suchness there is neither self nor other than self.

To come directly into harmony with existence, simply say that nothing is separate and nothing is excluded. No matter when or where or how, following the Way means entering this truth. And this thought is beyond extension or diminution in time or space, as it is a single thought in eternity.

To the master, the universe always stands before your eyes as infinitely large and infinitely small: no difference, for definitions have vanished and no boundaries are seen. So too is it with your Being and non-Being. Don't waste time in doubts and arguments, but move along and intermingle with all things without distinction. To live in this realization is to be without anxiety about non-perfection. To live in this faith is the way to non-quality because the non-dual is one with the trusting mind. Truly, the way is beyond language, for in it is found the great truth that in reality there is no tomorrow and there is no today.

– Translated by Ormond McGill

Something to think about...

Spear Seminar held at Ahn Taekwondo Institute
(Cincinnati, Ohio)

The Best Martial Art Quotes

"Looking Back to the Past While Moving Ahead to the Future."

That quote use to be on almost every flier my schools ever gave out. I thought it was very important to maintain our connection to the past without getting stuck in it and I wanted everyone to know that. On a personal training level I also wanted to live by that quote. For the most part I think I have. I still teach relevant material that I learned when I was a child but I also teach material that I have recently "adjusted" to how I know it should be taught now. I am, for the most part, not saying that the material I use to teach was wrong. It is simply wrong for the type of students I have today. Gone are the students that are happy standing in a horseback stance for 45 minutes doing front punches.

"The Wheel of Time turns, and Ages come and pass, leaving memories that become legend. Legend fades to myth, and even myth is long forgotten when the Age that gave it birth comes again." — ROBERT JORDAN

Recently I have been spending a lot of time cleaning in order to get ready for the arrival of several my students. While cleaning I happened to see one of my first journals. For those of you that don't know, I journal everything. Studying a lot of martial arts can be very difficult in the beginning if journals are not kept. One art tends to blend into another art and what a mess things can become. Anyway, I opened the journal and realized it was filled with quotes that I thought, at the time (keep in mind I was a child/teenager), were important, significant and worth saving. In this article I would like share some of these with you so that you too can hopefully find inspiration in them.

The first entry was in December 1979. (Quotes are not in order, a lot are skipped – the journal is an inch thick and filled with quotes. A lot of these quotes were taken from movies, which I loved as a child. Unfortunately, I do not know where a lot of these come from. Back then I was not really concerned with such things.

- If there is no contention, there is neither defeat nor victory. The supple willow does not contend against the storm, yet it survives.
- When you can learn to understand your own motives and the motives of your enemies, then you cannot help but win.
- True insight cannot be gained by specialized knowledge, by victory or defeat, by doctrine or dogma. It can only be achieved by the illumination of ones own inner self. Therefore, it does not matter who wins or looses.
- When one eye is fixed on the destination you have only one eye to search for the way. Concentrate on the now.
- However solid a building may appear, it is worthless if its foundations have not been well laid.
- One can become like a centipede that, in trying to figure out which foot moved when, ended up in a heap – paralyzed.
- The tree which the arms cannot encircle grew from the tiniest sprout; the tower of nine stories high rose from a small heap of earth; the journey of a thousand miles began with the first step. – Lao Tzu
- He who reigns within himself and rules passion, desires and fears is more than a king. – John Milton
- Ours is an age in which partial truths are tirelessly transformed into total falsehoods and then acclaimed as revolutionary revelations – Thomas Szasz
- Formerly, when religion was strong and science weak, men mistook magic for medicine; now, when science is strong and religion weak, men mistake medicine for magic. – Thomas Szasz
- How wondrously supernatural, and how miraculous this! I draw water and I carry wood! – P'ang-Yun
- We receive three educations; one from our parents, one from our schoolmasters and one from the world. The third contradicts all that the first two teach us. – Montesquieu

- Anything that is deliberate, twisted, created as a trap and a mystery, must be discovered at last. Everything that is done naturally remains mysterious. – Robert Browning
- The only true law is that which leads to freedom, there is no other. The only difference between the master and the student is that the master has begun to understand what he really is and has begun to practice it. – Richard Bach
- One is taught in accordance to one's fitness to learn.
- Development of the mind can be achieved only when the body had been disciplined.
- Seek not to know the answer but to understand the question.
- ... there is no education which one can get from books and costly apparatus that is equal to that which can be gotten from contact with great men and women. – Booker T. Washington
- ... the thing to do, when one feels sure that he has said or done the right thing, and is condemned, is to stand still and keep quiet. If he is right, time will show it. – Booker T. Washington
- If on a journey, you wish to rest in the shade, sit under the shadow of the big tree.
- Learn the ways to preserve rather than destroy. Avoid rather than check; check rather than hurt; hurt rather than maim; maim rather that kill; for all life is precious, nor can any be replaced.
- The way of the monkey is to play the fool. While you laugh at his antics, he bites you from behind. Unmask his ego and you expose a coward, disguised as a monkey.
- He is dead already. – Grandmaster Gallano

Something to think about...

Wooden Weapons Crafted by Author

If you don't have time to do it right, when will you have time to do it over?

In less than a week, I will be setting out on my 3.5 hour car ride to Camp Gorham in order to teach the 2011 Black Belt Winter Retreat. This will be the 20th retreat and it has been 10 years since it has been held at Camp Gorham (New York). There is a poem called "Deer Park Hermitage" that I often quote to my students because it holds the distinction of being my favorite poem. Most of my black belts know that it holds that distinction; however, I don't think any of them realize why. During the very first winter retreat I ever hosted, there were only 6 black belts in attendance. It was a strict meditation retreat – no talking and 10 hours of sitting meditation a day. Toward the end of the retreat, the black belts needed to be exercised, so I decided that we would climb a nearby mountain (mountains in NY are not really mountains they are just called that – more like very large hills compared to the Rockies). Once we finally got to the top, we found a clearing with a small rise in its center and one tree. While my black belts were enjoying their time not sitting in front of a wall and having way to much fun talking, I sat down in the snow and continued my meditation practice while looking out over the surrounding area. As always, while meditating, stray thoughts entered and left my mind. However, it wasn't just a random thought that entered my mind that time, it was the "Deer Park Hermitage" poem. I just sat there as the words of the poem flowed through my mind. No thought other than the words. Then when they faded, noting but emptiness – clear mind. The impact of that experience can't be put into words. There is so much contained in that poem that is so relevant to martial art practitioners. In the future I hope to talk about the individual lines and the "hidden" meaning of each of them. Until then, enjoy:

Deer Park Hermitage

So lone seem the hills; there is no one in sight.
But whence is the echo of voices I hear?
The rays of the sunset pierce slanting the forest,
And in their reflection green mosses appear.
-Translated by W.J.B Fletcher, 1919

Something to think about...

Pictures of the Grand Canyon taken by Author

Get Rid of the Clocks in your Bedroom

How many of you wake up to an alarm?

Over the past few years, I have only been woken up by an alarm two or three times (after traveling and changing time zones). The rest of the time I have woken up on my own. "Why does it matter?" you are probably asking. When we sleep, we go through various phases of sleep from very light to very deep. When you are woken up from a deep phase of sleep (by an alarm clock or a person) you will feel exhausted, even if you have gotten enough sleep. On the other hand, if you wake up when you are in a light phase of sleep, you feel refreshed and not sleepy, even if you didn't get enough sleep. In other words, the key is to wake up when you are in the light phase of sleep. This cannot be done with a conventional alarm clock because it has no idea what phase you are in. There are new alarms on the market now that can keep track of your sleep phase and only wake you up when you are in a light phase. That's great but why would you want to spend all that money on something that you don't need. With a little practice it is very easy to set your "mind" alarm clock. Simply tell yourself what time you want to wake up at and poof that is when you will wake up. Now it wont be exactly the time you "set", but it will be close and you will be in a light sleep phase. So, if you need to be up at say 6am, tell yourself that you need to be up at 5:30. That way you will have a 30-minute buffer. In the beginning, you will need to set your alarm as a backup, but within a week or two you will no longer need it. The only time I ever set an alarm is if I have to catch a very early flight, but I never need it (I set it just in case). At my winter retreats, I have to be up before 4am to get ready to ring the bell, never once in 25 years have I used an alarm. Every day I go to work I get up without an alarm. **It's not difficult**.

How many of you wake up on a daily basis and look at the clock to see what time it is? Those of you that do, how many of you decide to get up or stay in bed based on what time it is, instead of whether or not you are truly sleepy?

Ok, I realize that if it is a workday you need to know what time it is but on a non-work day do you really need to know? Why not simply get up when you are done sleeping? You might surprise yourself on how much your sleeping habits change simply by not looking at the clock. There was an interesting study done where several people lived in caves by themselves. They were told to sleep when they were sleepy and get up when they were not. Because they were in caves and they had no clocks, they had no idea what time it was and no idea how much time had passed. All of the participants in this experiment very quickly started sleeping less and less. Haven't you ever woken up fully rested only to realize that it was earlier than you had thought, then you forced yourself to go back to sleep and when you finally got out of bed you were exhausted? This is very typical occurrence.
Give it a try and see how much your life changes for the better.

Something to think about...

8 Quick Tips

오십일

Tip 1: There is a pause between Stimulus and Response.

In another article I posted about the transition that occurs between um changing into yang and yang changing into um. Basically I put forth the argument that they don't immediately go from one to the other. There is a transition phase between them. This phase can be very short/small or it can be very long/large, but it exists.

Recently, I have been teaching a lot of time management classes and inevitably when I do, Stephen Covey comes up. As I mentioned in a previous post, Covey has had a huge influence on my classes. Anyway, I recently was looking up something in Covey's "Eighth Habit" book and came across a concept of his that I had forgotten about: "There is a pause between stimulus and response". Covey believes everyone is born with the gift of choice. He puts forth the idea that when there is a stimulus, there is always a pause before the response and that pause, he argues, allows us to use this birth-gift of choice. The pause might be really short due to genetic, physical, mental, environmental influences but it exists and therefore there is an opportunity to make a choice before "response".

I don't agree with his choice of using the word "pause" because that would imply there is a stop between stimulus and response (um and yang). As I pointed out in a previous post, there is no pause/stop only a transition. That being said, this is a very important concept that everyone should learn. Everyone needs to take responsibility for their actions and realize they always have a choice because there is always a period between stimulus and response.

Tip 2: If One's Words are no better than Silence, One Should Remain Silent

How many times have you overheard someone talking about something you are knowledgeable about and they don't have a clue about what they are talking about? It happened to me last weekend. I was watching my wife's daughter playing in a soccer game. In front of me, was a group of three people. One person was going on and on about what a chiropractor can and can't help people with. Now, let me be clear, I'm not a chiropractor. One of my best friends is however and I am fully aware of the range of his practice.

This all started when the person talking (the talker) had mentioned that she had taken her daughter to a chiropractor. Her friend then said she was thinking about taking her daughter in for a condition she had. The "talker", who had no idea of what she was talking about, started telling her that chiropractors can't fix or help with that condition. Which is ridiculous, because my friend fixed the same condition in me. So what should the talker have done differently? She should have said, "I don't know if a chiropractor can help with that." "I'm no expert but if I had to guess I'd say they can't help with that." or "I have no idea if they can, but this is how my daughter made out with her visit." By acting like an expert, the "talker" basically convinced her friend not to take her daughter to a person that could have helped her. Who knows how long it will take before her condition is better now. It has been my experience that people who truly know what they are talking about don't go around talking about it and the people, who don't know what they are talking about, talk about it all the time.

So, if you have no idea what you are talking about, do everyone a favor and remain silent. I'm silent all the time (well most of the time).

Tip 3: a Life Lesson

> *A man was struggling in the woods to saw down a tree. An old farmer came by, watched for a while, then quietly said, "What are you doing?"*
>
> *"Can't you see?" the man impatiently replied, "I'm sawing down this tree."*
>
> *"You look exhausted," said the farmer. "How long have you been at it?"*
>
> *"Over five hours, and I'm beat," replied the man. "This is hard work."*
>
> *"That saw looks pretty dull," said the farmer. "Why don't you take a break for a few minutes and sharpen it? I'm sure it would go a lot faster."*
>
> *"I don't have time to sharpen the saw," the man says emphatically. "I'm too busy sawing!"*
>
> - Story from Stephen Covey's book
>   'THE 7 HABITS OF HIGHLY EFFECTIVE PEOPLE'

When was the last time you sharpened your saw?

Tip 4: Executing a Perfect Taekwondo Stance

A large number of Taekwondo Stances require the practitioner to have one or both of his/her feet pointing straight forward. A large number of practitioners use their big toe as an indicator of whether or not the foot is straight. Herein lies the problem. If the big toe is pointing straight forward, the foot is not. Instead, point the second toe straight forward. If it is straight, so to is the foot.

Tip 5: Executing a Perfect Taekwondo Stance – Part 2

This tip can drastically increase the stability of your stances. A large number of martial artists spend all their time focusing on the position of their feet (see last tip), the weight distribution between their feet, and the exact location of their feet relative to each other and their body. You might be asking, "What else is there?" Your tailbone. In every stance your tailbone has a very specific location it should be pointing at and if it is, your stance's structure (and balance) will be significantly improved. Typically, in a stance that has a weight distribution of 50/50 between the feet, the tailbone should be pointing to a spot at the middle of a line connecting the two feet. It wouldn't be practical to go over the tailbone position for every stance, but this should give you enough to experiment with.

Tip 6: Getting Pressure Points to Really Work

Students will often comment that a specific pressure point they learned isn't working. Typically, they assume that they are off in its location and sometimes they are. However, most of the time they are simply not "activating" it correctly. Some points need to be struck, some points need to be pressed and some need to be rasped to achieve the desired result. So, if a point isn't working, try the other two ways of "activating" it and see if one of them works.

Tip 7: Commitment

This is a quote from W.H. Murray that one of my instructors gave me in the 80's:

> *Until one is committed there is hesitancy,*
> *the chance to draw back, always ineffectiveness.*
> *Concerning all acts of initiative (and creation),*
> *there is one elementary truth, the ignorance of which*
> *kills countless ideas and splendid plans:*
> *that the moment one definitely commits oneself,*
> *the Providence moves too.*
> *All sorts of things occur to help one*
> *that would never otherwise have occurred.*
> *A whole stream of events issues from the decision,*
> *raising in one's favor all manner of unforeseen incidents*
> *and meetings and material assistance,*
> *which no man could have dreamt would have come his way.*
> *I have learned a deep respect*
> *for one of Goethe's couplets:*
>
> *Whatever you can do, or dream you can, begin it.*
> *Boldness has genius, power, and magic in it.*
>
> - W.H. Murry

It was very motivational to me and I hope it is to all of you as well.

Tip 8: The River

Wondrous beyond measure the great way. It flows off into nothingness like a vast river. When a newcomer arrives on its banks, he stands in awe at its majesty.

When a weak newcomer enters the currents of the great way he is overcome by its incredible strength and quickly leaves out of fear of helplessness, never to return again.

When an average newcomer approaches the currents of the great way he immediately looks for a downed tree or piece of land toward which to swim. Then very cautiously he enters the currents. Spending a considerable amount of time fighting them in order to arrive at his predetermined "safe" tree or piece of land, he tires. When the "safe" destination is finally reached, he barely has enough energy to pull himself out of the currents. Exhausted, and inspired by a fear of drowning, he swiftly departs, never to return again.

When a strong newcomer enters the currents of the great way, he fearlessly swims into its center, where the current is the strongest. Being content with the direction in which the current flows and never trying to change directions, he never tires. He is completely unafraid and surrenders to the great way. Occasionally, when the current leads into a downed tree or the shore, without hesitation he will dive back out into the current's center.

Every so often, even a strong newcomer will make the mistake of leaving the currents to circumvent a downed tree. Once he has left, a myriad of distractions will present themselves making it almost impossible to enter the current again.

Meeting a Master of the Way on the Way.

> If you meet a Master of the Way on the Way,
> Greet him neither by bowing or not bowing.

Over the past few weeks I have been thinking a lot about manners. As a student of several martial arts, I have come to appreciate that each art has something to offer. There are no bad arts or good arts, just arts that each teach us something different or teach us the same thing differently. Back in the early 1990's, I started practicing Kyudo (The Way of the Bow). For those of you that don't know, Kyudo is Japanese Meditative Archery. I am very fortunate to have a very gifted instructor, Shibata Sensei XX. He has taught me more than I can ever put into words, but all of his teachings can in part be summarized with one word, manners. When a person practices Kyudo, they cut through thinking mind with the sword of the shot and they are therefore able to see their true nature. The problem that most students don't realize is that the shot might be the teacher of the student, but the manners are the teacher of the shot. Perfection of the shot can be achieved only when manners have been perfected. Without manners there is no shot, or if there is a physical shot it is an illusion and the teaching of the shot is delusion. If I learned anything from Kyudo it is that true manners are one of the most important lessons that any martial art instructor can teach.

Through manners we are able to practice our art in such a way that the inevitable outcome is a disciplined mind. A disciplined mind allows for the development of a disciplined body. That in turn disciplines the mind to a greater degree and that in turn disciplines the body to a greater degree.... The cycle continues and compounds the beneficial gains over and over. However, it all starts with manners.

When a student first starts taking Taekwondo, they are taught the foundations of the art's manners. They are taught how to bow, how to address and interact with their instructors, they are taught the various ceremonies that make up a typical class, etc. Every time they go to class these manners are reinforced through both positive and negative motivation, and with time these manners become part of the student. Unfortunately, a great number of these students' manners are illusions, even though they don't realize it. They go around playing the role of a student that has good manners, fooling themselves and their instructors, unawares of this simple truth that what they are doing is a sham. It is true they are not to blame but unfortunately, they will never reap the benefit of true manners in their practice.

So who is to blame? The instructors are of course. Students are a reflection of their instructors. If an instructor has a bad quality, it is reflected and amplified by their students. Therefore, if an instructor's manners are an illusion, so are all of their students' manners. No matter how hard an instructor might try, they cannot teach something that they themselves do not possess. It would be like trying to reflect your brown hair, as blonde, in a mirror when you stand in front of it.

So, I ask all of you that are reading this, how will you greet a Master of the Way on the Way?

Something to think about...